# HEALING IN THE WORKPLACE

A Spiritual Guide to Coping with Work Issues

L'Orangerie Crawford
&
Terri Harrison

WestBow Press
A DIVISION OF THOMAS NELSON
& ZONDERVAN

Copyright © 2015 L'Orangerie Crawford & Terri Harrison.

All rights reserved. No part of this book may be used or reproduced by any means, graphic, electronic, or mechanical, including photocopying, recording, taping or by any information storage retrieval system without the written permission of the publisher except in the case of brief quotations embodied in critical articles and reviews.

The names used are fictional. And resemblance to actual persons, places, or situation is entirely coincidental.

WestBow Press books may be ordered through booksellers or by contacting:

WestBow Press
A Division of Thomas Nelson & Zondervan
1663 Liberty Drive
Bloomington, IN 47403
www.westbowpress.com
1 (866) 928-1240

Because of the dynamic nature of the Internet, any web addresses or links contained in this book may have changed since publication and may no longer be valid. The views expressed in this work are solely those of the author and do not necessarily reflect the views of the publisher, and the publisher hereby disclaims any responsibility for them.

Any people depicted in stock imagery provided by Thinkstock are models, and such images are being used for illustrative purposes only. Certain stock imagery © Thinkstock.

ISBN: 978-1-4908-5455-7 (sc)
ISBN: 978-1-4908-5457-1 (hc)
ISBN: 978-1-4908-5456-4 (e)

Library of Congress Control Number: 2014918119

Printed in the United States of America.

WestBow Press rev. date: 2/13/2015

# CONTENTS

I.     ACKNOWLEDGEMENT ......................................................ix

II.    INTRODUCTION................................................................xi

III.   WORK LIFE BALANCE.......................................................1

- THE MONEY CHASER ...................................................2

- THE CARE TAKER SYNDROME .................................7

- THE TRAVELER................................................... 11

- THINGS TO PONDER ON .........................................16

IV.    DECISION MAKING IN BUSINESS ...............................18

- SUNK COSTS ...............................................................20

- LENDING AND BORROWING ..................................25

- SCALING AND DOWNSIZING..................................30

- THINGS TO PONDER ON .........................................34

V.     UNPROFESSIONALISM IN THE WORKPLACE............36

- GOSSIP.................................................................37

- THE OFFICE CLOWN .......................................42

- DRESS CODE .....................................................48

- THINGS TO PONDER ON.................................53

VI.    LACK OF MOTIVATION FOR UPWARD MOBILITY...56

- THE PROCRASTINATOR ..................................58

- FEAR OF FAILING..............................................63

- FEAR OF ACHIEVING........................................68

- THINGS TO PONDER ON.................................74

VII.   NEPOTISM .................................................................76

- KINSHIP ............................................................77

- SPOUSAL SUPPORT .........................................81

- FAVORED EMPLOYEE.......................................84

- THINGS TO PONDER ON.................................88

VIII.  LEADERSHIP .............................................................90

- TRANSFORMATIONAL VS. TRANSACTIONAL....92

- TRANSPARENT LEADER ............................................96

- FAIR AND JUST LEADERSHIP .................................99

- THINGS TO PONDER ON .......................................103

IX. ORGANIZATIONAL CLIMATE ....................................105

- HAZARDOUS WORK ENVIRONMENT................106

- WORKPLACE VIOLENCE .........................................110

- PERSONALITY DIFFERENCES ................................114

- THINGS TO PONDER ON .......................................118

X. THE SOCIETAL OUTCAST ...........................................121

- CRIMINAL RECORD AFFECTING
  EMPLOYMENT............................................................122

- PERSONAL IMAGE AND WORKABILITY .............128

- THE NOT SO RETIREE .............................................131

- THINGS TO PONDER ON .......................................135

XI. INTERNAL WARRING ..................................................137

- BETTER YOU THAN ME ..........................................139

- BELIEF SYSTEM CHALLENGED WHEN
  MAKING DECISIONS .................................................143

- SPEAKING OUT AGAINST INAPPROPRIATENESS ............................................. 147

- THINGS TO PONDER ON ......................................... 150

XII. -ISM'S IN THE WORKPLACE ..................................... 152

- AGE-ISM .................................................................. 154

- RACE-ISM ................................................................ 158

- SEX-ISM ................................................................... 161

- THINGS TO PONDER ON ......................................... 164

XIII. MANAGING CONFLICT .............................................. 167

- EMPLOYEE/SUPERVISOR CONFLICT ................... 169

- EMPLOYEE/EMPLOYEE CONFLICT ...................... 173

- EMPLOYEE/CLIENT CONFLICT ............................. 177

- THINGS TO PONDER ON ......................................... 180

XIV. SERVANTHOOD ........................................................... 183

XV. BIOGRAPHIES .............................................................. 187

# ACKNOWLEDGEMENT

We would like to first and foremost give the glory and honor to our Lord and Savior, Jesus Christ for giving us special gifts and talents and for calling us to write this book. We would also like to thank our godson and godbrother, Brandon Rachel for connecting us to the Hokes family. We would also like to thank Pastor and First Lady Hokes for guiding us spiritually and for encouraging and inspiring us. To our home pastor, Bishop Frank L. Stewart of Zoe Christian Fellowship, we thank you for giving us spiritual foundation rooted in the five- fold ministry. We would also like to thank our family and friends for their uplifting words, reassurance, and support. We love you all. To our sister and aunt, Mimi Harrison, you have always been our cheerleader, giving us confidence even when we sometimes doubted ourselves. Your upbeat spirit can make the most cynical person a believer. This book is dedicated to our lovely mother and grandmother, Flossie Mae Harrison. You have been the rock that strengthens us all and the glue that holds us all together. We love you for your unwavering support. Thank you to everyone that purchases this book. We pray that you allow God to move in your lives.

# INTRODUCTION

The workplace has become increasingly complex to manage in recent years. For both supervisors and employees, differences in experience, personalities, and background often make it difficult for them to coexist. The workplace is a source of chronic stress for many causing negative outcomes such as absenteeism, low work productivity, sexual harassment, and workplace violence to name a few. Unfortunately, the woes of the workplace have become so common that many people feel helpless and hopeless and do not know how to handle workplace issues. In particular, many Christians do not know how to cope with workplace problems because they do not know how to deal with these issues from a faith-based perspective. To better understand the intricacies of the workplace, it is first important to understand why God has ordered us to work in the first place. The Bible discusses how God ordered us to till the land as a result of sin; however God does not want us to view the idea of work as a curse. Instead, He wants us to use our work performance as worship toward Him. When we dedicate our work performance to God, He blesses us beyond belief with things like promotions, favor with our boss, and an increase in pay. However, He never said that work would be easy. In fact, as Christians, we will face many challenges at work; many of which will test the very foundation of our faith. This is why God wants us to rely on His word when we come across those seemingly impossible to overcome obstacles on our jobs. The unfortunate part about this is that many Christians do not know where to begin when it comes to depending on God to help them with their work dilemmas. They may start with prayer and even seek the counsel of other Christians, but many are stuck after that. The reality is that there are things that we can do beyond prayer and seeking counsel to becoming victorious over our work problems. God gives us specific directives and instructions in His word on how to overcome work issues, but it is up to us to find the answers. This book helps us find those long awaited answers to the various work quandaries by using practical, every day scenarios and shows us how the commitment to following Godly principles will manifest life changing outcomes. Further, following these principles will help us to persevere through any storm at work and prepare us to be of help to those whom have been broken because of their work troubles. God wants us to allow Him to minister to us with His healing grace and mercy so that we can experience a fulfilled and balanced work life.

# WORK LIFE BALANCE

Work-Life Balance is the unique idea of stabilizing one's career and lifestyle. Some of the things that must be balanced between career and lifestyle are one's ambition to obtain more wages or a higher ranked position at work meanwhile desiring more quality time with family and friends, and maintaining physical, mental, and spiritual health. Balancing work and life, by all intents and purposes is not easy since many people have found themselves in a conflict between their work aspirations and personal life. When there is conflict between the two, a multitude of problems can occur. Some of these problems include a break down in physical health with stress being a contributing factor to high blood pressure and other cardiovascular diseases, and the emergence of anger, anxiety, and depression deteriorating one's mental health. More importantly, once these problems arise as a result of an imbalance in work and personal life, the "spiritual man" is gravely impacted and compromised. In fact, one of the consequences of ineffective work-life balance is the weakening of the relationship with God. Imagine working a job in which you compromise going to church and being fed with God's word to do overtime. You may initially justify this by telling yourself that you give tithes and offerings to your church and by acquiring more money would allow you to continue to give more tithes and offerings. You may even talk yourself into believing that watching Sunday morning church services on television before you go to work is suffice. However, you have failed to remember that God expects us to fellowship with others in the body of Christ. If this pattern of choosing work over your personal relationship with God continues, you may find that it becomes more difficult to hear God and once this happens, a vicious cycle is likely take place. If it becomes harder and harder to hear God because we have neglected our relationship with Him and have put other things before Him, we are likely to become angry with Him and stop seeking His face. Our spiritual lives are all about balance and maintaining stability. When there is a rift in how we balance our work and the quality of life and the things that keeps us happy and healthy, we are out of order with God's will for our lives. Surely, God wants us to be prosperous, successful, and hard workers. In fact, the Bible says in several passages that Jesus and God worked. John 5:17 states that Jesus answered the sick man at the Pool of Bethseda: "My Father has been working until now, and I have been working". This suggests that God expects us to work since we are created in His likeness. However, the Bible does not indicate that we must work at the expense of maintaining healthy physical bodies and certainly not at the expense of our relationship with Him. Issues in work-life balance can come in many different forms. Some people place higher emphasis on leisure and neglect their obligations to their jobs while others value their work duties more than their quality of life. The reality is that work-life balance is a concept that has been examined and analyzed for decades and with the way that the economy has shifted in recent years, it is fair to say that work-life balance will be an ongoing issue to come.

## Scenario - THE MONEY CHASER:

*Winston is a 44 year old man who holds a high ranked position at one of the top law firms in the country. In fact, his life's dream came true last year when he made partner. Winston has worked his whole life to achieve such a feat from joining the junior achievers club in high school magna cum laude at Stanford University Law School. Winston's job quite naturally causes him to work long hours; many of them going into the late night. This has contributed to extreme conflict with his wife,*

*Marie of 12 years. Winston and Marie have three children together; Charles, 10, Annabell, 6, and Justin, 3. The children are involved in several school projects and extracurricular activities that Winston has missed because of his work schedule. When confronted by Marie about his long work hours and lack of presence in the home, he balks by saying "you know how important this job is to me....I'm making sure that we get to take vacations to the Bahamas every year, that the kids go to the best private schools, and that you get to drive that Mercedes sitting in the driveway". Marie, dismayed by Winston's anger walked out of the room. Winston's pursuit of money and prestige within his firm has been an ongoing issue in his marriage. Although, his work schedule is tearing his family relationships apart, he justifies it by telling himself that his father was this way and this is all he knows. Torn between his zealous for his job and his love for his family, Winston is at a lost and does not know what to do.*

Many people are faced with juggling the demands of their job and family. Once more, many people like Winston place more worth on their work achievements and gaining money than appreciating the time that they have with their families. While others do not have the control of scaling down their work hours to spend quality time with their families as a result of the threat of layoffs and cutbacks because of the economic downturn, individuals similar to Winston have several things within their control to uphold the relationships with their families while giving their services to their jobs. It is important to note that while it is admirable to be ambitious and consider oneself as the "model" worker, there are many things that become disregarded when the focus is solely on achieving status and money at work. When this happens, one of the most important things in our lives that become ignored is family. The first thing that someone in this predicament must do is look within themselves and sincerely ask if there is a change that needs to be made. One of the ways one could do so is by assessing how other things in their lives have declined as a result of the disparity in the amount of time that they spend at work versus the amount of time spent at home. Though people tend to be awakened to their contribution to the deterioration in a relationship once the relationship has been severed, there are usually several warning signs that we receive prior to loss of the relationship. In Winston's case, his wife Marie has informed him several times that his lack of presence in the home has impacted her and their children; however Winston has chosen to ignore her warnings. This has become a problem because it appears that Winston and others similar to him are in denial. We are often in denial when there is a problem because it is too difficult to face the part that we play in someone else's unpleasant feelings toward us; however looking within oneself to examine faults is the first step in changing a negative behavior. Once people look within themselves, they can see how God sees them and the expectations that He has placed on them. It is important to understand that historically, men have placed a higher value on work considering that they were the primary breadwinners of the family for generations. The shift came; however with the emergence of World War II when women were faced with providing for their families while the men fought for their countries. Furthermore, it is acknowledged that with the growing trend of single parenthood, women are more and more placed in the position of being the head of the household. Though women being the primary breadwinners due to World War II and due to single parenthood have been unavoidable, God expects men to take on this role if they have made a commitment to their wives and children. Although men and women are now working at an equal rate, women are traditionally prone to placing higher value on family life. Since men have the ingrained propensity to find their worth at work and what they do for a living, it is essential that they understand how God sees their role in the family. It is normal, especially for a man to find his worth in his job. In fact, society has programmed men to evaluate themselves against one another by the jobs that they have, their statuses, and how much money that they have in the bank. Though this makes for healthy competition among men to acquire the finer things in life, God expects men to find their worth in their families as well. In fact, He lays out

*Healing in the Workplace*

specific rules that He requires men to follow when they gain a family. One of those rules is to make their presence known in the home. Psalms 78:5 states that the appointed law in Israel was that God commanded fathers to make themselves known to their children. It is impossible for children to truly know their fathers if most of their time is being spent at work. Furthermore, fathers have a responsibility to guide their children; particularly during their formative years when they are so susceptible to the attacks of Satan. Pastor Hokes suggested that fathers are the children's compass and they mustn't replace their presence with presents. All too often parents give their children material goods in hopes that it will make up for their absenteeism in the home. However, this only underlines and reminds neglected children of the unlovable feelings that they already have of themselves, thus causing strain on the parent-child relationship. Another expectation that God has for men as head of the household is to listen to their wives and hear what they are saying about the conflict and break down of the family since women tend to be the primary overseers of the family. A man who does not listen to his wife about what she has to contribute to the growth of the family is behaving foolishly in the eyes of the Lord. Men also must understand that God has called them to fix problems within the family with the assistance of their wives. Heading a healthy and happy family is much like any successful NBA team. The head coach cannot win games without listening to his assistant coaches whom often spend more individual time with the players than the head coach. Once men like Winston begin to see themselves through God's eyes and realize their role as the head of the household, they can then implement strategies to have a more balanced work and personal life and improve upon their relationships with their families. One of the things that they can immediately apply is planning schedules that include time with family and committing to that schedule. First Lady Hokes suggested that implementing weekly family nights to play games and interact with one another not only helps men to unwind but gives children long-lasting memories. It may also help to keep track of their schedules by using calendars. This way, if family night is listed on a calendar for every

5

Wednesday, for example, it is easier to stay committed to the obligation to the family. Another useful strategy for men whom spend more time at work than at home is to schedule weekly talks with their wives where each of them are listening to one another. Often times, there is conflict in relationships because we are not listening to one another and ignoring the other's needs. It is crucial for the family for the father and the mother to keep the lines of communication open and address and attend to each other's needs. Pastor Hokes often reminds couples whom he counsels that relationships are not one-sided and men whom seek their validation at work frequently feel devalued at home. It is important for wives to be open to hearing such criticism if their husbands are not receiving positive feedback and validation from them so that they can find solutions and make the relationship better. Creating long-term goals for the family is another necessary approach to improving work-life balance. For people like Winston, there is no problem is developing long-term goals for self which is why they have achieved the success that they have; however setting long-term goals along with the family is the only way to establish a legacy within the family. Fathers must sit down with their families and map out where they would like to be as a family in 5 to 10 years from now. This creates structure in the home and builds a bond within the family. One of those long-term goals should be to commit to going to church as a family on a regular basis. This leaves a legacy with the children that they are God-fearing and loving people and they can instill this value in their children when they become adults. It is a man's duty to ensure that his family is intact financially, mentally, physically, and spiritually. If any one of these things are unequal in relation to the other then the man is out of order with God. Men need to know that they have God's DNA within them which means that their affirmations and talents to be successful workers were given to them by God. Therefore, it is their duty to cultivate these gifts, talents, and abilities at work but understand that there is no good in profiting the whole world at the risk of losing himself and his family.

*Healing in the Workplace*

## Scenario - *THE CARE TAKER SYNDROME:*

*Joseline is a young, attractive, funny, outgoing, and kind woman living in San Francisco, California. She is a registered nurse in the pediatrics units at a small, private hospital near her home. Joseline comes from a long line of care professionals. Her grandmother is a retired nurse from Corpus Christie, Texas, her father is a clinical psychologist working with adolescents and her mother is an English teacher at an inner city school in Richmond, California. Joseline is the eldest of four children and has always been the "second mother" of the family from changing the diapers of her baby sister to rejecting a scholarship to attend college in Florida to stay close to home to help take care of her ailing grandfather. Aside from being helpful at home, she often extends herself to her colleagues at work which leaves her exhausted by the end of the day. One day, a colleague who was late to work asked her to cover her shift until she arrived at work. Joseline was fifteen minutes away from finishing her shift and thought that her colleague would surely be at work by the time her shift ended. Little did she know that the colleague was in heavy traffic and did not show up until 30 minutes after Joseline's shift ended. Joseline was very upset but when the colleague arrived to work, she just smiled and told her that she was happy to help her. When Joseline arrived home, she was still upset but instead of dealing with her feelings, she opened up a brand new carton of Rocky Road ice cream from her freezer, began eating, and watching reality TV. This has been a pattern for Joseline all of her life. Instead of setting boundaries when she is being taken advantage of, she acquiesces and is left stuffing her feelings. Joseline's lack of self-care has contributed to her weight gain of 45 pounds over the past 5 years and migraine headaches. Joseline appears happy on the outside but is unsettled internally. She often turns to her friends for guidance but is frequently disappointed by the advice given.*

Care professionals frequently have a difficult time balancing their work and personal life. Many people who go into care professions have big hearts and want to help as many people as they can. If it was not for these type of people, the world would be an even uglier place to live. However, while care professionals give their all to their jobs and to others on their jobs, it is often at the expense of their own well-being. There is truly nothing wrong with giving to others and in fact, we teach our children to give so that they won't become selfish adults. Nevertheless, if we give at our own expense, we are sending the message to others that we can be easily taken advantage of.

Being a servant to others is pleasing to the Lord. He expects us to cheerfully give unto others as He gave His only son to us. One of the most commendable qualities to have as a colleague is to serve. However, many of us can take things too far when we are giving without the expectation of reciprocity from others and when we give at the expense of our healthiness. First Lady Hokes called these type of people: "people pleasers". Some might question and even counter this by suggesting that it is Godly to give to others; however God does not say anything about being a doormat. As a matter of fact, God even does not like being taken advantage of and becomes angry with us and feels unappreciated if He senses that He is doing all of the giving in our relationship with Him without us giving anything in return. In order to find better work-life balance, it is first important to know what is driving someone to please others at their own expense. The scenario suggests that Joseline dislikes her "people pleasing" behavior yet she does not do anything to stop it. In fact, she internalizes her guilt of not speaking out against being taken advantage of by overeating which resulted in an extreme weight gain. This is a common problem that people have which is why it is important to get to the bottom of what is bothering them. It appears that Joseline and those with similar problems lack of confidence within themselves. There could be a number of reasons why they lack confidence. Childhood traumatic events such as parents' divorce, abuse, or being made fun of by peers at school can have a major impact on

*Healing in the Workplace*

someone's lack of confidence. These people appear to have it all together on the outside and can even deceive others into thinking that they are happy. However, when you look closely you can see a pain that is unimaginable. One of the reasons why people tend to overly give of themselves to please others is the fear of rejection. We all have had this fear at some point in our lives; however it becomes a problem when it stifles our quality of life. This fear also becomes problematic when we fail to acknowledge the acceptance that God has given us once we became a part of His kingdom. In the Bible, I John 4:8-11 states that God so loved us that He gave His only begotten son to the world and that we did not love Him but He loved us. God's abundant and overwhelming love for us is the greatest counter to this fear of rejection from others. The fact that God loved us before we even knew Him tells us that we are worthy. Another explanation for "people pleasers" is that they are often critical of the blessings that God has given them in their lives. When one is unhappy and prone to depression, it is easier to see the negative things in life rather than focusing on the positive things that God has given. Besides, this is out of line with God because though He requires us to be humble, He also expects our lives to be examples for others and wants us to give our testimonies about His goodness in our lives. If we continue to criticize and/or downplay the things that God has allowed us to accomplish out of fear that others will not like us, we are not spreading the word of how good God is to His children. Another rationalization for the "people pleaser" is the attempt to feel a void in one's life. Pastor Hokes explained that "people pleasers" often have a void in relationships and are seeking a connection to others. "People pleasers" tend to have superficial relationships which is why they desperately seek intimacy in their lives. Once "people pleasers" discover the drivers to their behavior, they can start to set boundaries with others. Setting boundaries with others; particularly when we are seeking their approval is a difficult thing. Still, it is necessary to keep ourselves safe. Imagine that setting boundaries is like building a fence around us. We can build this fence with a door that opens and closes which symbolizes the ability to give an opening to those who we want in our space and a closing to those whom we want to keep away. Setting boundaries also teaches others how to treat us. Once more, setting boundaries helps others to be independent and rely on God. Pastor Hokes eloquently told a reoccurrence of a story told to him by his wife, First Lady Hokes of when she was a small child helping her grandmother raise chickens. He said that his wife told him that she and her cousins would try and help the chickens hatch their eggs by cracking the egg shells. He said that she told him that they thought that if they put a crack in the egg shells then this would help the hatching chicks come out of the egg quicker. She told him that her grandmother got mad at them and shooed them away and told them that the baby chicks need to struggle to come out of the egg on their own to build strength. She also told him that the chicks that they helped come out of the egg did not survive while the one's that they did not help lived. Pastor Hokes gave this analogy to point out that "people pleasers" unknowingly take on the role of God and step in to help others but God's plan is for people to depend on Him. He also said that people need challenges and struggles in their lives in order to recognize that God is their answer and not man. Surely, God will place others in our lives to help us; however He wants us to know that we have to seek Him first. "People pleasers" have to balance knowing when it is time for them to help and when it is time for them to step back and allow God to move in other's lives. Once more, the "people pleaser" has to build more positive relationships with others and learn to receive in order to improve work-life balance. These people need to know that it is alright to receive from others. God even likes to receive from us through our praises and joyful noises unto Him. Understanding that there is a balance in giving and receiving in meaningful relationships will help "people pleasers" to better balance the giving and receiving in their work and personal lives. Finally, "people pleasers" need positive coping skills such as healthy exercise, journaling their thoughts, and even joining support groups. There is no greater desire from God for us than to know Him and know ourselves through Him. God wants us to know that we belong to a royal lineage and that we are worthy of

*Healing in the Workplace*

His love. He needs us to know that we have to command respect from others as His children and that although He made us to be relational beings, the only person we are required to please is Him.

## Scenario - THE TRAVELER:

*Roxanna and her family moved to Pomona, California last year, approximately 40 miles from her previous home in Culver City, California. She and her family were previously living in a small condo and were becoming crowded due to the new addition to the family. Roxanna is a single mother with three children; Zackary, 7, Ryan, 14, and Caitlin, 17. Caitlin just gave birth to a beautiful baby girl and is no longer with her high school sweetheart, the father of the baby. Because of the growing family Roxanna knew that she needed more space but couldn't afford to buy a bigger home in Culver City. She makes a relatively decent salary as a child social worker for the County of Los Angles but does not receive any child support from her ex-husband, the father of her children. One day, Roxanna's friend gave her the telephone number to a realtor who specializes in real estate in Pomona. Roxanna called and met with the realtor but was reluctant because she believed that her children would want to leave their friends. Additionally, she has seniority on her job and leaving to find a job in Pomona was out of the question. Though, Roxanna was initially apprehensive about potentially moving to Pomona, she found a home that she instantly fell in love with. It was four bedrooms, two car garage, two bathrooms, and a huge backyard for a very inexpensive price. The home was a "fixer upper" but she was willing to take the risk because she loved it so much. Shortly thereafter, Roxanna put in an offer and it was accepted. She and her family moved into the new home and she kept her job in Los Angeles and was now traveling 30 miles to and from work for a total of 60 miles per day. The LA traffic became increasingly stressful for her. She was more distant from her coworkers with whom she previously had a good relationship and she began snapping at her children when she got home. Everyone around her was noticing a change. On the road, her anger was palpable. She frequently used expletives toward fellow drivers when stuck in traffic and has even come close to causing several accidents on the road by cutting off others when she is angry. Roxanna's stress and aggressive behavior has become out of control and she is now having thoughts of moving back to Culver City.*

Commuting has and always will be a hot button topic of discussion as it relates to work-life balance. Individuals whom work from home have the advantage of avoiding heavy traffic, long traveling hours, and are more likely to stay connected to their loved ones. However, if you are anything like the majority of the population, you have to commute to work. In addition, if you live and/or work in a metropolitan area, you are likely to have a lengthy commute both to and from work. It is necessary to utilize effective strategies to balancing personal and professional objectives when traveling long distances to work; however countless people have difficulties achieving such balance.

Depending on the amount of time, traveling to work can be a breeze. Some people have the comfort of traveling only several minutes to work by car while others can walk to their jobs. Conversely, with the increase of this unstable job market, people have to ultimately consider keeping their jobs to maintain their lifestyles and finding a job closer to home is highly unlikely. Since it is highly improbable to find a job near one's home, people have to consider the costs when traveling to work. Most people consider things like the growing gas prices and cost of maintenance for cars when commuting yet many people fail to deliberate on the cost of travel on one's physical and mental health. Several studies have shown that traveling long distances to and from work can lead to unhealthy eating habits, heart disease, stress and anger issues. Once more, if mishandled, long commutes can seriously impact the relationships with family and friends. Although commuting to work is often necessary for us to make a living and maintain our households,

*Healing in the Workplace*

we must earnestly consider its' impact on our lives. God does insist that we do some traveling for work and business purposes. As a matter of fact, there are several stories in the Bible that reference Jesus traveling long distances to do His father's work. In Luke 24:13-21, the word of God talks about how Jesus traveled with two men to the village of Emmaus after He was risen from the dead. In the passages, the men did not know Him, but His purpose for the travel was to show those whom did not believe that He was indeed alive. This illustrates that God does call us to travel for our occupation; however what is most important is that we know if it is His will and not our own. Too many times we make a move without consulting Him. We make a decision based on emotions and impulse and never consider whether or not God has given us the vision and orders us to move. This is especially real in the case of Roxanna and those whom are in the same quandary. Roxanna moved and fell in love with a home in which she believed would be beneficial to her and her family. However, because of the move, she is now dealing with extreme stress and anger problems because of her long commute to work. Surely, Roxanna had good intentions when deciding to move her family to a home with more space; but it is quite possible that she did not wait to hear from the Lord and see if this was His plan for her and her family. God is constantly speaking to us but we frequently ignore His voice and because of this we do not know the direction that He has for our lives. He has a blue print for us and if we do not seek His guidance on what He wants us to do and where He wants us to go, we often miss out on the blessings that He already had in store for us. God does not want us to be impulsive in our actions but rather wait on His leadership to guide us. God's word gives us numerous of consequences that can happen if we move too swiftly without Him. He says in Proverbs 14:15 that he who is slow to wrath exudes great understanding but acting impulsively exalts folly. This means that we are foolish if we are quick in our actions and responses to situations but God honors those whom are level-headed and collected in their thought process. God, however does understand that we are imperfect people and that there is no one on this earth whom has not acted quickly and foolishly at least once in their lives. Nonetheless, He demands that as we mature in the body of Christ, we have to exert some control over these impulses and wait on Him to tell us what to do. Much like anything that we want to master in our lives, we have to practice this skill but it can be done. In Roxanna's case, it would have been more advantageous for her to wait to hear from God to see if moving to Pomona and traveling a long distance to work was in the blue print for her life. God also tells us that if we wait on Him and turn our ears toward Him, there will be no stress, anger, nor anxiety once He has given us the word to move. Unfortunately for Roxanna and many of us whom have turned our ears away from God, we have to deal with the negative consequences because of our disobedience. Pastor Hokes suggested that when God gives us direction in our lives, there is no anger and anxiety because He promises to take care of us if we are obedient to Him. In addition, God gives us favor wherever we are positioned. In fact, He sometimes wants us to reposition things in our lives. In other words, it is quite possible that Roxanna did not need to move to an entirely new city to achieve the things that she wanted but rather she should have reevaluated and repositioned some things in her life to make her house a home. God may have only wanted her to cut back on her spending habits or pay down some outstanding bills to make things more comfortable for herself and her family rather than moving altogether. However, she would never have known this if she did not ask God and wait to hear from Him. Pastor Hokes advised that God can make any place our Canaan if He anoints it and gives us favor. Since God promises this to us, we have no business moving without Him. The great thing about the God that we serve is that even if we move without His consultation and consent, He can turn things around in our favor. One of the things that God can do if we move too swiftly is give us revelations on what to do to come out of our dilemmas. People whom are traveling too far of a distance to work and are exhibiting stress and anger as a result can do things to make it better. One of the most important things to start off with is to plan out one's day before the day even starts. This can happen by getting up a little earlier than usual and mapping out the

*Healing in the Workplace*

commute and planning for things like heavy traffic. Although traffic is out of our control, planning multiple and alternative routes to and from work can help ease stress and anxiety. Another strategy to use when commuting long distances to and from work is utilizing tools to manage the stress that comes with the travel. Effective relaxation tools to de-stress are to listen to soothing music and/or practice deep breathing exercises during the commute. In addition, having and maintaining an exercise regime is a great way to reduce stress. Learning to decompress when coming home from work is highly crucial in maintaining one's sanity. People must talk to their children and significant others about what is needed for them to be their best when they get home. One of the things that people can do is sit down with their families and tell them that when they get home from work every night, they will need some quiet and alone time for roughly 15 minutes to unwind and then they can attend to their needs. This helps the children and spouses empathize with the commuter's situation while helping the commuter feel supported. On the same lines, commuters must build a support network through family, friends, and/or church members to fill in any gaps in their absence. For example, if the commuter will be late in picking up the children from school, it would be beneficial for the commuter to seek assistance from a family member or friend to pick up the children and take them home. In addition, the commuter can stay connected to the family by leaving little funny and sweet notes for the children before leaving the home for work as a way of keeping his or her presence in the home. Lastly, when God gives us direction for our lives He promises to give us all of the necessary information and tools needed for the move to be successful. This means that we will have all of the resources available to us to ensure that His plan for us will not fail. First Lady Hokes suggested that commuters must ask God what their resources are in this situation. For example, she recalled a time when she had a long commute from home to work and she asked God to point her in the right direction for resources. She said that she saw a commuter's hotline telephone number on a sign on the freeway, called it and found a woman who was traveling to the same area where she worked every morning. She said that they soon began commuting together and it cut down on the wear and tear on their cars and they were even able to travel in the carpool lane cutting down on the time spent in traffic. First Lady Hokes explained that she would have never known about this resource if she had not asked God to reveal the information that she needed to know to make her travel to work anger and anxiety free. God guarantees that He will never forsake us and even when we are operating against His will, He continues to stay faithful. We must know that God wants us to practice listening to Him and not acting impulsively. He promises that if we seek His face for the blue print of our lives, we are promised blessings beyond comprehension. However, if we are disobedient and act on our own merit, we will have consequences to bear, but He still can turn things around to work out in our favor.

## THINGS TO PONDER ON:

- The word of God promises the children of His kingdom that if we are tithers and cheerful givers then there will be no lack in our finances, thus we do not have to chase money. Have you adopted the Godly principle of tithing and giving?........Malachi 3:11

- God designed families to support one another. Neglecting one's family to chase money can put a dreadful strain on relationships and can sometimes go without repair. Often times when one does decide to put family before the pursuit of money, it is too late to repair the relationship lost with them. God tells us that a consequence of our selfishness may be that we do not get a second chance......(The story of Ananias and Sapphira) Acts 5

- Often times, "people pleasers" have a difficult time expressing their feelings to others in an honest manner. This goes against God because He suggests that a Godly relationship with others

*Healing in the Workplace*

is built on open and honest communication. When we hold back on expressing our feelings and needs to others, we are not being transparent. Even Jesus was transparent with God on the night before he was set to die when He expressed His concern to Him about dying. Are you open and honest with those around you or do you keep your feelings inside out of fear?.......Luke 22:39-46

- When we look to others for validation instead of looking to the Lord for our identity, we start to compare ourselves to others. This comparison to others can lead to developing a jealous spirit but God actually expects His children's lives to be an example to nonbelievers......Romans 10:19

- Are you traveling without a purpose? God puts us in positions where we have to go long distances to build character and trust in Him. Think about Moses traveling the dessert for 40 days and nights. God had Moses travel for a purpose as well as God knew how much Moses could bear. God will never have us go on a journey not knowing how much we can physically, mentally, and spiritually take. He will bring us out of our journey once He knows that His purpose for us is fulfilled and we have reached our breaking point.....1 Corinthians 10:13

- Commuting long distances for a long period of time can lead to the sacrifice of healthy choices. Far too often people overlook the healthiness of exercise, sleep, spending quality time with family, and spending quality time with self. We must know that if we are choosing a path that sacrifices our health and well-being, then we are going against God's will for our lives..... Genesis 2:2-3

# DECISION MAKING IN BUSINESS

People make decisions on a daily basis from deciding on what outfit to wear to work to making decisions on what breakfast to eat in the morning. Our lives are saturated with decision making yet we tend to take this process for granted. Decision making is important because it is the foundation of making judgments. Judgments is an extension of decision making; however it differs because it involves identifying something based on a value. In other words, we all make judgments about objects based on whether or not we perceive those objects to be "good" or "bad". For example, consider that you are in the process of buying a new car and you narrow it down between two different cars. You might value one of the cars as "good" because it has central air and heating and a V6 engine, but you might judge the other car as "bad" because it has none of the things that you are looking for. Decisions are the outcomes of the judgments that we place on things. Therefore, since you made a judgment on the two cars, you then are better equipped to make a decision on which one to buy. Decision making is crucial in business; especially for leaders because it provides them with the tools needed to do the right things for the business. There is never an easy way to know if you have made a right decision as a leader; particularly if you are making decisions on your own. Furthermore, the ability to make decisions is based on our own outlook on the situation which is why business leaders are always encouraged to make decisions with

*Healing in the Workplace*

others when it is necessary. The reason why it is important to include others in the decision making process as business leaders is because making decisions by oneself is likely to lead to decision errors. When we make a decision, we are biased because of our own preferences, but other people can help us see things from different perspectives. This is especially important for business leaders whom live a Christian lifestyle. God wants to be sought out for guidance even before a decision is made. Proverbs 16:33 suggests that every decision is from God and if we are making decisions on our own, it can lead to serious consequences for our businesses. God does understand that being in a position of leadership sometimes means that we cannot consult with just anyone about a decision which is why He instructs us to surround ourselves with likeminded people whom have our best interest at heart. Once more, He does not expect us to make daily business decisions on our own unless He has given us specific directives to do so. Even Jesus understood that He was not called to do His work alone and solicited twelve disciples for help. What is important about this is that Jesus called upon these men because they each had individual qualities that would help Him as the leader and the ultimate decision maker of the group. God wants us to recognize that He has given other people special gifts and talents that we can benefit from when making decisions, but it is up to us to recognize how these gifts and talents can be married with our vision. Once more, it is advantageous to include likeminded people in the decision making process as leaders because it makes it easier to brainstorm ideas and solve problems if they arise. Decision making; particularly in business is not an easy task. If we make poor decisions because of our failure to hear from God's instruction then it can lead to catastrophe. However, He wants us to know that although decision making can be difficult, He is there to give us direction and He also places likeminded individuals in our path to help us when needed.

## Scenario - SUNK COSTS:

*Back in a small town in Georgia, Verdell and LaShawn are a married couple who own a small hardware store. The store was in Verdell's family for generations beginning with his grandfather who opened the store after the end of WWII. Verdell's father took over the store but died three years ago and left it for Verdell and his wife to manage. Since his father's death, the hardware store has incurred a significant amount of debt. Distributors of merchandise have increased their cost and inflation has gravely impacted business. The store is the only one of its kind in town which is a good thing but because Verdell and LaShawn are operating by themselves they often can't keep up the demand of their customers. On top of that, a mass hardware distributing warehouse in Atlanta has been interested in contracting with them to supply some rare goods to their customers. This would mean that they would have to mail their goods to the warehouse. LaShawn was thrilled about this opportunity because it meant that it would be another stream of income for the business and would help the store grow. Verdell, on the other hand was adamant about keeping things the same and not changing the way his father and his grandfather operated the business. LaShawn responded to him by saying "this is an opportunity from God...don't you see that"; however, Verdell insisted to keep business as usual. Growing tired of the couples' indecisiveness, the large Atlanta warehouse rescinded their offer. Now, Verdell and LaShawn are in a bind not knowing what to do with the business. LaShawn has become so angry with Verdell that she is considering moving to California to live with her sister.*

Sunk cost is a business term that refers to a business leaders' emotional tag to a decision at the expense of the business. Additionally, these poor decisions often lead to a price that cannot be restored. One of the most important things that we must know as business owners when we are faced with making tough decisions is if we are operating in God's

*Healing in the Workplace*

perfect will. Since we know that God has a blueprint for our lives, we have to gain an understanding of what He wants us to do when making business decisions. This means that we cannot make a judgment about a business opportunity until it is confirmed by God. This is especially true for Verdell in the scenario because he should not have valued the opportunity to expand his business as a bad thing until he sought God's face and waited for confirmation. Most times, we are too afraid to seek God's face on a decision because we are too focused on what things look like in the "natural" and forgetting that God operates from the "supernatural". It is quite possible that Verdell did not seek God's face on the decision to expand his business because he was too concentrated on the increasing debt that his store acquired. We must understand that God allows our businesses to go through rough patches because He wants us to put our trust in Him. Pastor Hokes said that he continuously encourages others whom are discouraged when making decisions to read Proverbs 3:5-6 which states: "Trust in the Lord with all your heart and lean not on your own understanding". He said that people need to be reminded of this scripture because God looks different to them in the signs of trouble than when things are going well. He recalled in the Bible when Jesus calmed a storm, walked the waters and called Peter to come out and walk with Him. The Bible notes that Peter was afraid but God had perfect confidence that Peter would be fine. Pastor Hokes gave this analogy because God wants people to know that He is there reaching out to us during signs of trouble even if we do not recognize that it is Him. We quite possibly stall on making decisions for our businesses because we do not recognize that it is God who has placed an opportunity in our paths to help weather storms. This is because we do not look beyond the storm to see the calm after the storm. In addition to this, we are often afraid to make business decisions because we judge the outcome as being good or bad. Some people are afraid of failing which is why they tend to stay stuck and continue to conduct faulty business practices, while others are afraid of succeeding and neglect making decisions because of they are afraid of the added responsibilities that come when one succeeds. Pastor Hokes said that he likes to tell his congregation to give themselves permission to succeed, evolve, and mature with the times. Far too often, Christians are afraid to move with the times that they are in because they do not want to fall prey to things of the world. However, God instructed us to be in the world and not of it because we are to lead the world by the example of our lives, but He does understand that we have to move with the ways of the world in order to make ourselves accessible to others to win souls For His kingdom. For example, In the times of Facebook and Twitter, many ministers have elected to use these platforms to attend to the needs of the people. God understands that the world is now more technologically based and He wants us to learn these things in order to reach a wider audience when we are witnessing and ministering to others. Evolving with the times is essential to our businesses because it allow us to reach a mass audience. Furthermore, we must look at our businesses as ministries. Christians are not just in business to make money, but God has called us to minister to others through our businesses. He promises us that if we are in His will and in our purpose or our ministry, then He is obligated to open ever door of opportunity for us to be blessed and bless others. Verdell and business owners like him must know that God is not going to allow an opportunity to arise only to have it fail. God promises that His plans will be done. Furthermore, Verdell must recognize that his father and grandfather had business practices that were fitting for them during the times that they were living in. Therefore, those same business practices were more than likely not conducive for the times in which Verdell was living. God wants us know that we must keep our Godly principles but we must also change with the era in which we live. God has given us all different ministries and He assures us that He will open doors that fall in line with those ministries. Additionally, God places the perfect people in our lives to help us make those hard decisions for our ministries. He puts these people in our lives because He knows that we cannot do things on our own. He often wants us to delegate responsibilities to others whom are equipped to handle them because He knows that we cannot do everything on our own. Consider Jesus calling upon the

*Healing in the Workplace*

twelve disciples for His ministry. He not only knew that He needed help to advance His ministry, but He was comfortable with delegating various responsibilities to them. In Matthew 10: 1, the word states that Jesus gave the twelve disciples power over unclean spirits, to cast them out and to heal many sicknesses. Jesus was not intimidated by giving the twelve disciples power because He knew that this was the most effective way to advance His business. Verdell potentially opposed to LaShawn's input about the business opportunity because he may have been afraid to delegate responsibilities and allow her to have decision making power over the company. A business owner who does not acknowledge the input from the people whom God has placed in their lives and delegate responsibilities to them is going against God's very nature. Jesus and the disciples knew that He was called to make the final decisions, but He was not opposed to including them in the decision making process because He understood that including them made His purpose stronger. It only hinders our purpose when we are too obstinate to listen to the input of those whom work for us. Although a potential consequence of making decisions alone is destruction, God wants subordinates of leaders and business owners to pray for them and pray that God enlightens them on what to do. As subordinates, we must pray for our leaders even if they have turned opinions away and we do not agree with their judgments. In LaShawn's case, it would not have benefited her to engage in an altercation with Verdell about his decision. Instead, it would have been more advantageous for her to pray that he opens his eyes to God's will for the business rather than making the decision on his own. She also should have prayed that God speaks to Verdell and help him get to the underlying issue of his emotional tags to the business and why he operates the business the same way as his grandfather and father even though those practices are not beneficial for the current time. First Lady Hokes pointed out that Verdell's emotional tie to the business was possibly because he was grieving the loss of his grandfather and father. Furthermore, it is understandable that Verdell wants to maintain the essence of the family business; however it would have behooved him to communicate this to LaShawn. This is all the more reason why the couple could have benefitted from getting wise counsel. First Lady Hokes suggested that when making any major decision, we should seek wise counsel from those whom have gone through similar experiences and/or have the skills set to counsel. She explained that the Bible tells us that there is safety in great counsel. This is because that when we are seeking out counsel, we are really seeking the wisdom of others and God says that there is security in wisdom. This is even laid out for us in the book of Proverbs, beginning with the proverbs of Solomon which addresses knowledge and wisdom. In Proverbs 4: 11, the Bible states that the way of wisdom has been taught and leads to the right paths. This shows us that the wisdom of Godly counsel will lead us in the right direction. However, many of us are opposed to seeking counsel because we do not want to admit that there is an issue that additional help is needed for, or we have been taught to handle our problems on our own and not to "air out our dirty laundry". Each and every one of us have problems and need someone in our lives to talk to. The Bible says that in Job 16:6, Job answered his pitiless friends that his grief was not relieved and how was he to be at ease if he remained silent? This suggests that we all can benefit from talking to others about our issues in order to get some relief. One of the ways that Verdell and LaShawn could have sought out wise counsel was talking to others whom have been in business longer than them and have had to make difficult decisions with their businesses. In addition, they could have sought out business consultation from professionals whom are knowledgeable about effective business practices. Another way that the couple could have sought out wisdom was to enroll in business courses to expand their business knowledge and skills. There are many inexpensive courses or workshops that they could have taken from the local junior college. This would have helped them advance their knowledge in marketing strategies and leadership skills. One other option to seeking out wisdom would have been to scan the environment and look for similar businesses that are successful and gain an understanding of how they are conducting their business operations. In addition to this, Verdell and LaShawn would have benefitted from

*Healing in the Workplace*

having a business plan as a guide to address things such as a marketing plan, financial plan, and operational plan for the business. Business owners should never conduct business without a well thought out business plan, but they often do not have a clue on what this is. In this case, it is essential for them to solicit the advisement from a business professional. A good business plan should have the company's vision, mission, and purpose statements as a reference guide for business practices. Additionally, every major decision for a business requires implementing a strategic plan that includes a S.W.O.T Analysis which gives them a layout of their strengths, weakness, opportunities, and threats. If Verdell and LaShawn had a business plan, they could have used it to address how they were to deal with this business opportunity. Making a decision as a business owner is one of the most difficult things to do and even when we think we are judging things the right way, we still can have negative consequences. This is why God wants us to listen to Him and include people whom are in accordance with our ministry. We must know that we cannot make business decisions alone and we may even have to seek out the wise counsel from others. In addition, we have to know when our emotional ties to a decision is hindering us rather than advancing our purpose.

## Scenario - *LENDING AND BORROWING:*

*Lindsay and Katie are sisters from a town in the mid-west and own a popular cupcake bakery. Their specialized cupcakes and exceptional customer service have helped them become profitable over the past 8 months. Lindsey and Katie were asked to participate in a baking goods tradeshow in New York to showcase their products and expose them to a larger audience. The sisters know that this is an extraordinary opportunity and would be "all in" in a heartbeat; however, after paying their employees and paying the rent, they aren't left with enough money to pay for travel and booth expenses for the tradeshow. When the sisters explain this to their older brother, Ted, he tells them to borrow a loan from the local bank. They are reluctant to follow Ted's advise because of the remembrance of a daunting experience that their cousin, Lance had when he borrowed money to finance his auto parts shop. Lindsay and Katie are also confused because they remembered reading a passage in the bible stating that they should be the lender and not the borrower. Besides, they never have experienced working with a bank to finance their business given that they used their inheritance from their deceased grandmother to open the bakery. The pressure of this opportunity has become so great that the sisters are considering giving up and letting the business opportunity go.*

Financing one's business is always a source of stress for business owners. Some people are blessed with receiving grants while others have to seek out loans from the bank to finance their business. When business owners are faced with making decisions regarding finances, this can be an even more stressful time in their lives. God gives us standards to live by to help us work through financial matters yet many people still have challenges with making sensible financial decisions for their businesses. Many people have such trials because they do not know what the word of God says about dealing with finances and business. Furthermore, during stressful times, people are more likely to make a flawed financial decision because they are not addressing the problem in a practical way.

Making a judgment call on borrowing money to finance a business is one of the most significant decisions in business. When deciding to take out a loan, business owners have to ask themselves specific questions before making the final decision. Some of those questions include: "What is the loan needed for?" and "How long should the terms of the loan be?". This is a good start to making a decision on borrowing money, but it is not the sole basis of making the decision. First and foremost, people need an understanding of what God says about lending and borrowing. In the scenario, Lindsay and Katie recalled reading a passage in the Bible referring to God wanting them to be lenders and

*Healing in the Workplace*

not borrowers which is why they were reluctant to take out a loan from the bank, per their brother's advisement. Though this passage is true, the sisters completely misinterpreted what God is saying. The passage in Deuteronomy 15:6 does in fact state that God says that we shall lend to many nations and shall not borrow but He is not suggesting that we are going against His word if we have to borrow money to advance our purpose. What He is saying in this scripture is that He promises to bless us beyond our own ability to receive that we will have enough left to lend to others and not have to borrow. Pastor Hokes revealed that many Christians take God's word out of context because they are extracting things from it and adding their own interpretation rather than reading the text simply as it is. He went on to suggest that this is a serious problem for Christians because they can stifle their growth when they are misreading God's word. Furthermore, we can stifle our growth if we do not take the time to ponder on His word and ask God to give us enlightenment. Pastor Hokes recommended that when we are reading a scripture in the Bible that we do not understand, we must close the Bible and then ask God to inform us what He wants us to know from His words. Pastor Hokes also recommended purchasing Bible commentaries or different versions of the Bible that explain God's word in simpler terms. He said that using Bibles such as the New Living Bible can help us better understand the text. Another reason why many people do not gain a full understanding of God's word, thus misreading it is because they rely too much on hearing others quote the scriptures rather than taking the time to study the word on their own. We all have been in situations when we have heard our grandparents or parents quote Bible verses and it becomes so routine that we begin quoting these scriptures in the same way. This is faulty because God wants us to know Him and have our own personal relationship with Him; however how are we to do that if we do not take the time to study His word. Lindsay and Katie would have considerably benefited from gaining a better understanding of the scripture regarding lending and borrowing; helping them make a more informed decision on financing their business. The next thing that business owners need to acknowledge is that there is no business that operates without some type of financing. This does not necessarily mean that a loan has to be taken out but money is required to advance your ministry and purpose. Jesus even needed money to advance His business. In Matthew 17:24-27, Jesus needed to pay taxes for the upkeep of the temple in Jerusalem but He did not have the money. Jesus also needed the counsel of Peter to direct Him in the best way to obtain the money. He goes on to ask Peter if He needed to obtain the money from a family member or from strangers in which Peter told Him that it would be from strangers. Peter then goes to the sea, per Jesus' instruction and casts a hook to take the fish that came up first. The Bible says that Jesus told Peter that he will find money in the mouth of the fish. This scripture falls in line with the idea that we must have money to finance our businesses because if Jesus did not pay His taxes, then there could have been severe consequences for not doing so. This scripture is also important because it shows that Jesus relied on His relationship with God to provide the money to pay His taxes. Many times we do not know where to find the money for our businesses because we are not seeking God's revelation on where to go and find it. We usually follow our first instinct which is likely to take out a loan from the bank but God gives us many examples of how to obtain money for our businesses. Taking out a business loan from a bank may be out of the question because of various issues like poor credit; however God can help us through this too. Jesus did not have the money to pay His taxes, but that did not stop God from seeing Him through this dilemma. The scripture shows that when we trust in God and work with Him, He can come up with creative ways for us to obtain money for our businesses. In Lindsay and Katie's case, taking out a loan to finance their business opportunity may not have been the best option; however that does not mean that God wanted them to allow the business opportunity to pass by. First Lady Hokes said that there are some opportunities too big to pass up. Furthermore, Pastor Hokes suggested that the sisters could have asked for donations from customers, family, and friends to raise the money rather than giving up all together. Additionally, First Lady Hokes said that the sisters could have put their money together and find

*Healing in the Workplace*

inexpensive ways to go to the tradeshow like traveling by bus instead of by plane or staying with family members or friends, if they had any in New York to cut down on hotel expenses. Lindsay and Katie should have also devised and/or revisited their business plan to see what is says about their marketing strategy and their budget for marketing. Business plans are great tools for business owners to have because it helps put them back on track when heavy decisions are to be made. If the sisters revisited their business plan, they would have possibly found that they had strategies in place to finance such business opportunities. One other tip that the sisters could have followed is conducting a self-inventory assessment to identify their individual knowledge about debt. Many business owners do not understand the difference between good and bad debt. For example, taking out a loan to finance one's education is good debt because it helps the individual advance in his or her career, and he or she will be able to obtain a decent salary to pay the money back. However, having tons of credit cards and not being able to pay them off is an example of bad debt. God states that it is a fact that going into some debt is inevitable but He does not want us to be fearful of this. He; however wants us to weigh the cost when we decide to borrow money and understand that it is our responsibility to pay the lenders back. Business owners need to understand that the consequence of opening a business may be acquiring some debt, but God never said to allow this to stop us from moving forward with our purpose. What He expects from us is to have a plan to pay down our debt and depend on Him to handle the rest. God will always give us creative ways to acquire money if we are in concert with Him. He never said that we will not have to pay debt which is suggested in the Bible when Jesus had to pay taxes, but He does want us to know that we need faith and a plan to work through whatever financial concerns that we may have.

## Scenario - SCALING AND DOWNSIZING:

*Johnson's printing company is a large company that has been around for 30 years and has withstood some of the toughest challenges in business. However, the current challenge may be the toughest. Due the economic downturn, Johnson's is forced to scale down and possibly disband some of its smaller departments. Johnson's CEO, Mr. Locklee is saddened by this because he promised the founder of the company that he would operate the business under the principle of integrity, equality, and fairness. Although, he wants to uphold the founder's wishes, he knows that if the company does not make immediate moves to downsize, the company will fold. Some of the departments that Mr. Locklee is looking to downsize are comprised of employees whom have given 30 years of service to Johnson's printing. After scanning the departments, he realized that some of the other employees are young professionals whom he promised a bright future with Johnson's printing. After long days of consultation and sleepless nights, Mr. Locklee decided to let 15 employees go from two departments and then consolidated the now smaller departments into one large department.*

Businesses are constantly faced with changes whether it is changes in the industry or in the organization's culture. When confronted with such changes, business owners and leaders have to make decisions that impact themselves as well as their workers. One of the most difficult challenges that businesses face based on the changes in the environment is scaling and downsizing. Once more, there are many reasons why leaders must downsize such as the threat of competition or the ever so unpredictable economy. Whatever the reason, business leaders must know how to handle downsizing with tact and finesse considering that many of their employees' future with the company is hanging in the balance. God wants these leaders to know that even if layoffs and scaling down departments are inevitable, they still have a duty to these employees to send them off with dignity and respect.

*Healing in the Workplace*

Having to downsize departments is a common issue in business, yet many leaders do not know how to handle this with skill. Even further, many do not have the guidance from God to help them make appropriate decisions when scaling their businesses. Pastor Hokes reported that every leader has to deal with controversy and every Christian leader should always ask God for wisdom and knowledge when making difficult decisions. One of the most nerve-wrecking things about being a leader is making decisions that are unpopular among your subordinates. However, difficult decisions must be made. God knows that as we move up in rank, the spotlight gets brighter on us and the moves that we make are more scrutinized. This is why God wants us to lead by example in whatever we do. Business leaders have the difficult task of making decisions that may upset some of their employees all while maintaining dignity and grace. One of the most common reasons why leaders have to downsize and layoff people is because some employees are no longer a good fit for the company. This is distressing because most leaders hire employees with the intention of them being a good fit for the organization. Since downsizing may be the most appropriate option for some businesses, leaders must still maintain some sort of decorum when letting employees go. Jesus is the ultimate example of a leader maintaining dignity in the midst of controversy and having to layoff one of His employees. Jesus knew that Judas Iscariot was no longer a good fit for His ministry because he had agreed to betray Jesus which led to the plot to kill Him. Jesus even confronted Judas about this asking him in Luke 22:47, "Judas, are you betraying the Son of Man with a kiss?" This shows that Jesus knew at that point that Judas would no longer fit into His ministry. Once others around them saw what was going to happen, they asked Jesus if He wanted them to strike with the sword and even cut off the ear of one of the servants of the high priest. However, this was not acceptable to Jesus as evidenced by Him healing the servant's ear. This suggests that even in the midst of death caused by the betrayal of one of His workers, He still maintained His dignity. God wants business leaders to use Jesus' example of letting go of employees with dignity and respect. God also knows that making such decisions is never easy even if some employees are no longer helpful for the company. Pastor Hokes said that whenever leaders have to make difficult decisions, they will always have some anguish but this does not mean that the decisions should not be made. Furthermore, business leaders have a responsibility to let employees whom are to be laid off know that they were valuable to the organization even if it was only for a period of time. This is one way that business leaders can downsize with dignity and integrity. Laying off loyal employees is an even harder decision to make for business leaders because of the emotional attachment that some employees have to the company. Although emotional connections are common in business, sometimes sound business decisions must be made without having the emotional attachment. We have all heard the phrase, "this is business and not personal" and surely some people can take this too far by suggesting that there is never an emotional tie to business. However, often times emotional attachments can get in the way of making sound decisions and lead to decision errors. This is why many business leaders are encouraged to utilize effective business tools when hiring and/or firing employees. Many times employees are selected because the employer has a "good feeling" about them, perhaps because of the way that they dress or how eloquently they speak. Nevertheless, this is a faulty business practice because it has no bearing on how well an employee can do his or her job. One of the most effective tools for talent selection suggested to business leaders is the use of structured interviews coupled with employee assessment tests. This is a better way of getting to know prospective employees' strengths and weakness and therefore enables employers to make a wise decision on who to select for the position. Using effective tools such as employee assessments is even beneficial when making a decision to layoff an employee. One of the tools suggested to business leaders that Mr. Locklee could have benefited from is the use of the 360 degree feedback assessment. This assessment is a way to assess employees' performance level, job duties, and skills set and gives feedback on these things from the employee themselves, leaders, and colleagues. This would have helped Mr. Locklee see where his employees are in the company and determine who is no longer needed without allowing emotions to get in the way of making the decision. One of the ways in which Mr. Locklee could have given his employees integrity while letting them go was to offer a severance package and/or allowed them to cash in their sick leave. First Lady Hokes said that Mr. Locklee could have even given the employees letter of recommendations and even recalled when an employer did this for her when she left a job. Also, it would have benefited Mr. Locklee's employees whom were being let go to be given business tools such as a S.W.O.T Analysis and GAP Analysis to ascertain their strengths, weaknesses, opportunities, and threats as employees. The GAP Analysis could then be used to help the employees find steps to bridge the gaps between their strengths and weaknesses. This would have been a way to better prepare them for the workforce if laying them off was unavoidable. Furthermore, God wants employees whom have been laid off to know that they can still leave their current positions with honor and use those same skills learned from the previous position in a new position. One example of this in the Bible is when Pharaoh no longer considered Moses to be an attribute to the Egyptian kingdom. However, during his time spent with the Egyptians, Moses acquired special skills from them and God used Moses in a new position to deliver His people. This example gives us hope in knowing that the preparation given on one particular job is not banished just because we may have lost that job. God can always use those skills for different assignments. God is so faithful and promises to be with us no matter what our outcomes look like. Business leaders must call upon Him to give them strength when having to make difficult, yet necessary decisions such as laying off employees to sustain the company. Employees whom have been let go have to lean on God and ask Him what their next assignment is and be confident that their skills acquired in the previous job will not go in vain. God always promises us that if we rely on Him then He will see us through.

*L'Orangerie Crawford & Terri Harrison*

# THINGS TO PONDER ON:

- Are you stuck in a rut without any direction? One of the reasons why we find ourselves in a bind that we just cannot seem to get out of is because we do not seek wise counsel. God's word says that His people perish from the lack of knowledge. God expects us to attain knowledge so that we do not fail.......Hosea 4:6

- Going into business with someone else is sometimes daunting and even more overwhelming when it is with a family member. Regardless of it being difficult, God expects us to be committed to one another as business partners. His word shows us that when two or more come to an agreement for anything, it will be done by Him. However, if we are not in accordance with one another, then we are allowing conflict to impact our relationship........Matthew 18:19

- Decision making in business first starts with evaluating why we are going into business in the first place. God wants us to have a plan whenever we have to make business decisions especially as it relates to finances. He instructs us to write things down and make it plain, that way we will have a vision and take action toward accomplishing the vision...............Habakkuk 2:2

- Do you need to find creative ways to finance your business but have not asked God to reveal resources to you? God will give us insight into different ways to fund our purposes but we have to ask Him. Think about Joseph who was the business consultant to the Pharaoh because he had great business ideas. In Pharaoh's dream, it was revealed to him that there would be a famine. Joseph had the idea of taking all of the goods during the plentiful seven years to be stored for the famine. Once the famine came, all countries went to Joseph in Egypt to buy the

*Healing in the Workplace*

goods. Joseph was resourceful and used creative ways to meet the need of the kingdom.........Genesis 42:37-57

- What do your employers think of you as a business leader? Do they think of you as being fair and just, exerting an abundant amount of wisdom or do they think that you have poor leadership skills? Solomon was known for being a fair, wise, and just leader. One example of this was when he gave the baby back to his biological mother after he was stolen from her by another woman. Business leaders' decisions do reflect their leadership skills and how their employees view them........1 Kings 3:16-28

- Many times business leaders make poor decisions because they are looking for counsel in the wrong people. God has people whom intercede for us to help us make better decisions. Consider Esther who interceded to save the Jews. The story goes on to say that she fasted for this purpose and went on to reveal to the King the plot by Haman to kill the Jews. The King heard Esther's plea and had Haman and his children killed. This shows that because Esther was a God fearing woman, she was able to intercede on the King's behalf and appeal that he make a wise decision...................Esther, Chapters 3-7

# UNPROFESSIONALISM IN THE WORKPLACE

We all have either seen or heard of someone behaving unprofessionally in the workplace. There are times when we are focused on completing a task and a colleague will distract us by talking very loudly in the office or by using vulgar language. These situations not only affect the flow of productivity, but it can lead to detrimental consequences for companies. Some of the things that can occur as a result of unprofessionalism in the workplace is low employee morale, conflict, and high employee turnover. When all is said and done, the underlying reason why some employees behave unprofessionally in the workplace is because they have a lack of respect for themselves and others around them. Respect is something that we are taught in our childhood from our parents, teachers, peers, and other influential people in our lives. We are taught to respect ourselves and others by being given consequences by our parents when we behave poorly or even by witnessing examples of the adults in our lives whom treated each other with respect. If we were not taught respect as children, we are likely to treat others disrespectfully as adults. As a result of having inadequate examples and/or teachings of respect as children, many employees do not have the basic foundation to treat others with respect while on the job. On the flip side of this, behavior, even poor behavior is a choice meaning that we all can choose to behave poorly or properly. Each day that we go to work, we are faced with choices on whether to behave professionally or unprofessionally.

*Healing in the Workplace*

The mystifying part of this is that it is less likely that one will behave professionally if they were not given appropriate tools as children. This is why God holds all parents and other influencing adults in children's lives accountable for preparing them for the real world. Children must be guided on how to behave properly in the workplace even before they have a full understanding of the work environment. One of the ways parents can guide their children in being respectful and professional employees is by teaching them to be respectful and professional students at school. This means that they have to be taught to respect the authority of teachers and behave justly toward their peers. God says in Proverbs 22:6 that parents need to train their children in the way that they should go and when they become adults, they will not stray from those teachings. Our parents are our first examples of how to treat others around us in an appropriate manner; however as adults we still have a responsibility and a choice to behave correctly. James 4:17 suggests that it is a sin if we know to do good and choose not to. This is especially important for those whom are believers in Christ and continue to misbehave at work. God holds us to an even higher standard because we are to turn away from the wrongdoings that we engaged in before we were born again. If we behaved improperly at work by using foul language, undermining our colleagues, or being dishonest before we became saved, God expects us to let those things die once we have accepted Him as Lordship over our lives. Even though God gives us instruction on how to no longer engage in inappropriate behaviors, many of us are still tempted to misbehave at work. There are many things that colleagues and employers can do to combat and even prevent unprofessionalism in the work setting. However, it requires team effort and diligence to tackle this issue.

## Scenario - GOSSIP:

*At a medium size computer processing firm, Donald, Carol, Harper, and Analiese are a close knit team. They are responsible for the outputting of computer software systems. Due to the nature of the job, they often work on projects together. Because they are so close, they frequently share personal stories about spouses and children with one another. They also engage in water cooler conversations about their favorite TV shows and about the latest and juiciest gossip. They justify this behavior by saying that they are not only colleagues, but they are friends who hang outside of work. One day, Donald overheard a rumor about Barbara, the newly hired senior manager in the operations department. He overheard that Barbara is gay and has a domestic partner of whom she has been living with for over 10 years. Additionally, he overheard that she and her partner are in the process of adopting a child. Shocked by this information, Donald told Analiese about the rumor over their daily cell phone conversations after work. They both said that Barbara did not "look gay" and that they were surprised that she was hired by Barbara's boss who seems to be homophobic. The following day over a morning coffee break, the group were having their usual conversations about the latest celebrity gossip which included an A list actor coming out as being gay. This triggered Donald and Analiese to share the rumor about Barbara with the rest of the group. Unbeknownst to them, Barbara's supervisee was in a room nearby and overheard them talking about her. The supervisee was appalled by their behavior but was at a lost because if she was to tell, then she would be considered a gossip too. The supervisee decided to go to human resources and share what she overheard the group saying about Barbara.*

Gossip is one of the most common and unproductive misbehaviors at work. It can lead to the breakdown of communication, lack of trust among colleagues, loss of productivity time, and even legal ramifications. The unfortunate thing about gossip; particularly in the workplace is that almost all of us can admit to engaging in it at least once. Even if we know how unproductive it is, we sometimes cannot fight the urge to either listen to or provide someone with a "juicy" piece of gossip about our colleague(s). This behavior is utterly displeasing to God. In

*Healing in the Workplace*

1 Timothy 5:13, God calls people whom gossip "busybodies" and refers to them as being idle or lazy. Even Christians struggle with gossiping behaviors in the workplace; especially if it was an issue for them before being born again. The beautiful thing about God is that He knows that we all have infirmities, yet He still called us to be a part of His kingdom. However, He does not want us to use the fact that He called us even with our weaknesses as a reason to not grow and mature in our lifestyles as Christians. Pastor Hokes said that all Christians have and will have times in their lives when their previous sins will come "knocking at their door". Nonetheless, God wants us to come to Him and get delivered from those sins. Proverbs 28:13 says that a man who covers his sins will not prosper, but whomever confesses and then forsakes them will have mercy. God knows that some people struggle with gossiping at work, but He insists that we mature and ask Him to help us with this problem. Once more, as we are born again, we are required to be new "creatures". This means that we earn the right to witness to others through our lifestyles. How can we as Christians be a witness to our colleagues at work if we are the ones starting rumors about others at work? Once we become Christians, we become liberated from the things that previously held us in bondage. God does not want us to become entangled in the old things that we used to do, but stand fast and hold true to His word (Galatians 5:1). One of the many reasons why Christians continue to engage in misconduct; particularly at work even when they know that God disapproves of it is because they are often in denial. Pastor Hokes jokingly stated that many Christians suffer from "Deny-A-Betes". He said that denying one's misbehaviors and faults can become an infirmity in and of itself because it weakens the growth of our spirits. He also said that often times Christians know that they are engaging in something that is wrong but they are more concerned with maintaining a certain image in front of others. This is notably true for Christians whom like to engage in workplace gossip because they know that it is wrong but because they want to be liked and part of the "in-crowd" at work, they engage in it anyway. Another reason why many Christians engage in office gossip even when they know that it is sinful is because they have

39

not been confronted about their behavior from other Christians. As Christians, it is our duty to lovingly confront one another about our lifestyles if we are living contrary to how God wants us to live. When we are confronted about our misbehaviors is only when we become convicted and change our ways. Be that as it may, many of us do not want to be told about our wrongdoings because many of us do not want to change. Pastor Hokes suggested that many Christians like to be associated with religion but not with conviction. However, he went on to assert that Christianity is not a religion but it is a faith with standards of living. He also declared that Christianity is the only faith in which God pursues us while religion is in pursuit of God. This means that when we are born again through the body of Christ, God shows us the things that He has done for us to live right according to His principles. This supports the idea that we will only change once we already have detailed and outlined rules of living that we must adhere to in order to receive the things that He promises to us. When we live according to His standards is when we can receive His promises. God wants us to know that we cannot continue to talk and spread nasty rumors about one another at work but expect to be blessed. He wants us to know that our blessings come from living right with Him. Pastor Hokes eloquently stated that satisfaction and happiness are byproducts of righteousness. Therefore, no matter how much we are preached to about prosperity in church, we will not reap the benefits of His promises until we are living righteously according to His word. Additionally, receiving such messages about prosperity and gaining material goods is a trick of the enemy because God says that our souls must be first prosperous. It even suggests this in Mark 8:36 that for what will it profit a man to gain the whole world than to lose his soul? Our pursuit for happiness should not be in gaining worldly goods but in making our souls right with God. Only then will He promise us the gain of the righteous and then we will be truly happy. Have you ever noticed that people whom gossip are unhappy within? They are often motivated to talk about others because they are so unhappy with their own lives. Since gossip is a sign of idleness, it can also be referred to as being empty. Many people whom

*Healing in the Workplace*

gossip are empty inside and they only feel gratification when they are talking about someone else's misfortunes in life. We all have heard the saying that "misery loves company". This is principally true of those whom gossip about others because they are seeking to fill an empty void. Furthermore, it is sometimes easier to talk about someone else's life; particularly if they are going through hardships than to look at our own adversities. In the vignette, this may have been the case for the group who gossiped about their newly hired colleague. They may have been in some way displeased about their own lives and instead of focusing on themselves, they gossiped about their colleague's sexuality as being "taboo". Even so, one's sexuality should never be a "taboo" issue in the workplace because we must all learn to work with one another regardless of race, creed, and sexual orientation. God expects us to be able to work around people whom are different from us even if we do not live our lives the same way that they do. As a result of judging others at work because of their sexuality, we often lose out on learning from smart and talented people. In addition, this we can potentially find ourselves in legal trouble for discrimination if we are purposefully gossiping about them. Organizations are obligated to ensure that such consequences do not occur. One of the ways that the organization in the vignette could have handled this group's gossiping behavior was for human resources to meet with them to discuss the company's policy on misconduct and the severe consequences of defaming others. Another solution to this problem would have been for management to dismantle the group and transfer them to other departments. Disassembling groups whom gossip is a way to keep down unproductive behaviors at work and it sends a strong message that this behavior is intolerable in the workplace. Further action steps can be taken such as splitting up break and lunch times and giving written reprimands depending on the severity of the gossip. Organizations should also implement training that address gossip to give employees tools on how to interact with their colleagues in a more appropriate way. There are several things that colleagues can do to fight against gossip. One of the things that they can do is to ignore it and not feed into it by listening to rumors. They can walk away when they see

41

others gossiping or they can simply and politely tell others that they are uninterested in gossiping with them. Furthermore, if the gossip becomes severe enough that it begins to affect them, they can confide in a supervisor or do what Barbara's supervisee did in the vignette and talk to human resources. Some people are afraid to speak out against gossip out of fear of retaliation from the gossiping party or parties; however supervisors and human resources are obligated to keep their names anonymous when addressing the issue. The moral of this story is that gossip is ungodly, unproductive in the workplace, and can lead to grave consequences. However, there are many things that can be done to prevent and treat this issue. The persons whom gossip have a responsibility to recognize that this is a struggle that they are dealing with. They need to seek out help through trainings, guidance, or mentorship to work through this problem. Moreover, Christians whom struggle with gossiping in the workplace can seek out the guidance from a minister and can also ask God to remove this sin from their lives. Organizations can implement sensitivity training programs and follow up with consequences to help decrease gossip at work. Once more, employees can confidentially speak to a supervisor or human resources about this issue. Knowing that there are solutions to dealing with this problem can provide some comfort for those whom do not gossip at work. However, the ultimate comfort is leading by example by not engaging in this behavior even when enticed to do so.

## Scenario - THE OFFICE CLOWN:

*Derrick is a 29 year old receptionist at a digital animation company. He is friendly, extremely outgoing, and funny. He is also well liked by most of the employees in the office. Derrick is always asked by many of the employees to attend lunch mainly because of his entertaining jokes about people in the office. Although, Derrick is well liked, he has been written up twice by his supervisor for being too loud in the office and using company time to entertain the other employees. He has*

*Healing in the Workplace*

*acknowledged that his behavior should be toned down and has impacted his productivity, but he sometimes can't resist the impulse to make jokes at work. He particularly likes to talk about employees' style of dress and how they style their hair. Derrick has a particular obsession toward Candace, one of the company's animator. Candace likes to wear wigs and bright colored clothing. Derrick does not like Candace's clothes and the way that she dresses. He despises the wigs that she wears unknowing that Candace has alopecia. Derrick's jokes about Candace go over well with many of the employees except for Lisa. Lisa and Candace are not friends but Lisa feels sorry for Candace. One day after work she saw Candace in the parking lot and asked her how she felt about Derrick's jokes about her appearance. Candace confided in Lisa and began to cry and said that she was considering filing a complaint against Derrick. Lisa consoled her and offered her telephone number to talk.*

Telling jokes is another unprofessional behavior that causes negative chain of reactions at work. If the jokes are at the expense of one's colleagues, it can lead to conflict and altercations both verbal and physical. No one should ever have to come to work and be fearful that they will be made fun of or talked about in a negative way, yet the workplace is encumbered with this problem. Much like the class clown at school, the jokester at work is in constant pursuit of making his or her colleagues laugh, but what they do not understand is how unproductive this behavior really is. This type of misconduct in the workplace can lead to distractions, disruptions, and wasted time. Office clowns are usually well liked because they are funny and their sense of humor can lighten up intense moments; however they need to understand that there is a time and place for such behavior. Furthermore, these individuals actually have a lot of strengths and can use their sense of humor in more helpful ways. It is a positive thing to be funny; even Jesus had a sense of humor when communicating His message. Take for instance in Matthew 7:3-5 when He was talking about hypocrites whom judge others. He used a funny imagery of hypocrites looking at a speck in other people's eyes but ignoring the plank in their own eyes. Jesus intended for this analogy to be funny to get His point across. However, unlike many jokesters at work, Jesus knew how and when to use His sense of humor to relate to others.

As mentioned earlier, office clowns have the gift of making others laugh. Because of this, they are usually well liked by others because they are often entertaining and animated. People like to be entertained which is why we pay money to watch funny movies or go to the circus to see the tumbling gymnasts and amusing clowns. There is something fascinating about watching someone do something that you cannot do. With that being said, we are not always in a mood to be entertained. Sometimes we are in serious moods and need to be in serious environments. The problem with office clowns is that they are almost never in a serious mood and often take serious matters too lightly. One of the authors recalled a moment in church when her Bishop was ministering a serious word about someone dying and one of the churchgoers laughed in response to what the Bishop had said. This undoubtedly made the author uncomfortable, but it even made the Bishop uncomfortable as evidenced by him stopping the sermon and asking her what was funny. He also told her that he did not think that what he said was funny. Many times, office clowns take serious moments too lightly because they are uncomfortable with the subject matter being discussed and they cannot contain the inner anxiety that comes with listening and/or discussing sensitive matters. In addition, many of these individuals have yet to fully mature and they cannot handle serious matters. Pastor Hokes referred to these people as having "Peter Pan Syndrome" or the inability to grow up. He also said that in such situations, one has to think about these individuals' childrearing. Pastor Hokes suggested that people whom make jokes at inappropriate times or make others the brunt of their jokes were typically encouraged as children to be funny, but this gift was not cultivated in the appropriate way. He said that the parents of these individuals may have noticed that they had the gift of making others laugh but may have never talked to them about using it

*Healing in the Workplace*

to make people feel good and not feel bad about themselves. Moreover, parents should not encourage their children to be obnoxious and abusive toward others through their humor. Parents have a responsibility to talk to their children about being respectful toward others even in their joke-telling; otherwise they are prepping them to be obnoxious and verbally abusive toward their colleagues when they grow up. In fact, the ability to know when and how to use humor takes maturity. Regrettably, some people just do not mature. Pastor Hokes said that he believes that some people can be young in age for a time but immature forever. God desires that we become mature not just physically, but mentally as well. In 1 Corinthians 14:20, God's word says that we should be mature in our understanding. Part of being mature in our understanding is not thinking about things in a way that we did when we were children. Children, in their right are self-centered. Their self-centeredness is not intentional or with malice, but it just is. As children grow, their self-centeredness dissipates and they begin to think more about other people's feelings and how their behavior affects them. Some adults have not reached the level of maturity in their thinking to reflect on how they may impact someone else. This can be said of the office clown because often they do not exhibit the empathy needed to know when their jokes have affected their colleagues, nor do they understand when it has impacted productivity. Another sign of immaturity that office clowns exhibit in their thinking is not understanding when their jokes are and are not of value to others at work. It is certainly acceptable to use humor to make a positive connection with a colleague or coworker, but it must be done with grace. One of the authors thought about a time when she was working as a child therapist for an agency and often used humor to connect to her clients. She said that the children responded to humor and they eventually talked about their problems. She went on to say that she knew when and when not to use humor with these children because she knew that they were dealing with some serious matters. This example is supported by Ecclesiastes 3:1 which says that there is a time to weep and a time to laugh. Another cause contributing to people being the office clown is that they are often seeking validation from others in the workplace. Think about when children do something funny and they ask their mothers to look at them. When their mothers laugh at them, they feel a sense of validation and it helps to build their self-esteem. Office clowns are no different in that they frequently make jokes to receive validation from their colleagues. When their colleagues laugh at their jokes, they feel worthy. The problem with this is that we are not to seek our validation at work; we are to go to work to provide a service. Additionally, people have to consider that if they continue to tell jokes to receive validation from others, there may come a time when these same people begin to lose respect for them. Surely, we all want to be liked wherever we go but we should not go to work with the intention of being liked or being told that we are valuable. We all can agree that it is a wonderful thing if our colleagues or supervisors tells us how great we are, but God wants us to be sure of our greatness even if we are not told from others at work. Besides, He wants us to do our jobs unto Him and not for the purpose of pleasing others. Inappropriate jokes and teasing on the job is like a virus. It spreads and if fed, it becomes stronger and stronger and is uncontrollable. There are many things that can be done about this form of misconduct, but people need to be willing to not condone it. First and foremost, people often believe that to condone a behavior means to allow or accept it; however this is false. By and large, condoning one's behavior really means to disregard or ignore it. This is a genuine issue as it relates to misbehaviors in the workplace because far too often people ignore it in hopes that it will go away or because they simply do not want to get involved. However, overlooking verbally abusive teasing and uncomfortable jokes is problematic because it sends a message to the victim that this behavior is acceptable and it also suggests that they may have in some way asked to be talked about. It is never acceptable to discount colleagues' verbally abusive behavior for the sake of telling jokes. God demands that we witness to one another. Once more, witnessing to one another is not just about telling people that Jesus is alive and that He is Lord, but it also requires convicting one another when we have done wrong. This can be done by showing them Godly alternatives to conduct themselves in a more

*Healing in the Workplace*

appropriate manner. Much like Lisa in the vignette, we have a responsibility to one another when we are seeing each other in pain at the hands of someone's verbal abuse or joke-telling. We need to reach out to both the victim and the wrongdoer. It is certainly one's right to not get involved in this type of situation at work, but one must ask themselves if not getting involved is in accordance with God. God certainly does not want us to involve ourselves in such situations if it will gravely harm us; however He does give us ways to get involved without compromising our own safety. Genesis 4:8-11 gives us an account of when Cain killed Abel and attempted to hide it. When God asked Cain where Abel was, Cain responded with "Am I my brother's keeper?" What Cain did not rely on was God cursing him from the earth. God does require that we look out for one another but not wanting to get involved is contrary to His word. One of the ways in which employees can help those whom are being made fun of at work is to reach out to them and offer consolation. This act of support is not about choosing sides, but it is about taking a stand against this type of misbehavior in the work environment. Another strategy that employees can implement to fight against such behavior is to offer support to the wrongdoer through mentorship. It may seem senseless to reach out to people whom are misbehaving at work, but these are the people whom need the help the most. In fact, First Lady Hokes suggested that Derrick and people like him need training and that they need more mature coworkers to help guide them. She also said that it is never too late to receive training from others; however people should be mindful that their help may not be well received. Nevertheless, this should not stop us from talking to these individuals and offering our help. One of the ways in which organizations can reduce this sort of misbehavior is to introduce conflict resolution strategies with all involved parties. This will help decrease the risk of verbal and physical squabbles by giving them the necessary communication skills to prevent problems resulting from unwanted teasing. One other solution that organizations can employ if the office clown's behavior becomes critically harmful is for the office clown to be placed on Administrative Leave and be made to attend workshops and training on bullying in the workplace. In addition, if the behavior continues even after the person returns to work from Administrative Leave and having taken training on bullying, the office clown can be terminated. Organizations also have an obligation to protect the victim of the teasing by offering counseling through the Employment Assistance Program, if utilized by the organization. This will help the victim talk to a trusted and skilled counselor about his or her feelings and learn ways to better cope with the circumstances. This is mainly important in this day and age when many people do not have appropriate coping skills and retaliate in devastating and sometimes fatal ways. The victims need to know that their anger is comprehensible but revenge is never acceptable. Clowning around at work does not always warrant serious consequences. Some gentle corrections such as moving the office clown's workstation or asking him or her to limit this behavior to break and/or lunch times can help. Still, serious consequences need to be in place if this behavior does not stop.

## DRESS CODE:

*Chantel, a 24 year old woman, and Roger a 32 year old man both work for large organizations in their town. Chantel is bright, attractive, and energetic. Roger also has the same qualities. Chantel's organization has a strict dress code in which employees have to wear business attire from Mondays through Thursdays but are free to wear casual clothing on Fridays. Roger's organization, on the other hand does not have a strict dress code but he notices that the managers always wear suits. Roger aspires to be a manager one day but he likes the idea of wearing baggy jeans and sports jackets to work. Chantel likes to "spice up" her wardrobe by wearing large earrings and open-toe high heel shoes. She also likes to wear short skirts and low cut tops on casual Fridays. Chantel has a good relationship with her supervisor and is being mentored by her to move up in the company. However, Chantel's supervisor insists that her style of dress restricts her from advancing and contributes to her being overlooked for promotions for less talented employees. Meanwhile, Roger just cannot wrap his head around the idea of wearing suits everyday as he is comfortable with how he already looks and believes that promotions should be given to those whom are qualified and should not be based on how someone looks or dresses.*

Inappropriate clothing is another issue as it relates to unprofessionalism in the workplace. Many companies have policies and guidelines to monitor employees 'style of dress yet many of them do not follow the rules and they dress however they choose. It is understandable to want to dress according to one's personal taste, but a blatant disregard for companies' dress code policies is disrespectful and harmful to the work environment. People often take for granted that their style of dress in the workplace impacts organizations and clients alike. If someone dresses inappropriately at work, it sends the message that the person and the organization does not care about his or her professional image. Even if an organization does not utilize a specific dress code, employees have the responsibility in knowing what style of dress is appropriate for their industry and should take pride in their appearances. In addition, failure to take pride in one's appearance as a Christian is suggesting that we are not taking pride in God since we were made in His image. Once more, we are the light and are to be the example for others. However, if we as Christians dress inappropriately at work by exposing too much or wearing wrinkled and unclean clothing, then we send the message to the rest of the world that this is how God is since we are reflections of Him. We must ask ourselves this every time we walk out the door and present ourselves to the world: "Am I representing God in the best possible way?" If we can truthfully answer this question as "no" then we are out of line in the eyes of God.

Priding oneself in his or her appearance is one of the greatest things about being a teenager. We all can think back to those times in junior and senior high school when we spent hours in the bathroom, prepping ourselves to impress someone at school that day. If you are a woman then you can remember taking the time to straighten your hair and making sure that no strand was out of place. If you are a man then maybe you remember putting globs of gel in your hair to slick it down. Furthermore, if you are a parent of a teenager then you now know how your parents felt when they were trying to get you up and out of the house by a certain time but you could not resist the urge to look your best for the day. Taking care of one's appearance is all a part of growing up and discovering our unique styles. In fact, many have argued that the teenage years is when one should experiment with his or her hair color and style of dress. However, teenagers' style of dress should be supervised by adults. We would not dare let our teenage daughters go out of the house with a short skirt, exposing her underwear nor would we allow our teenage sons to leave, wearing jeans that show their entire backside. The irony to this is that some parents whom are up in arms about their teenage children dressing inappropriately for school often wear the same type of inappropriate clothes to their jobs. It is pointless to discipline one's child for dressing too provocatively or untidy if we as the parents are presenting ourselves in the same way to our colleagues and clients on a daily basis. Again, we know that children do as we do and not as we say. God wants us to understand that how we dress; especially in the workplace makes a statement. First Lady Hokes said that this is particularly true for women since they are being judged by others on a consistent basis. She said that she mentors the young girls in her church and encourage them to dress like young women by being modest in how much of their bodies that they expose. She also said that in 1 Timothy 2:9, God's word suggests that women in the church should adorn themselves with modest apparel. This scripture is not suggesting that women should not wear expensive clothing if they can afford to do so, but it is suggesting that women should be demure, especially in a professional setting. What's more, the hard truth is that women have been and may always be judged in the work environment. It is just how it is. However, women can do things like dressing professionally rather than provocatively to reduce some of the judgment

*Healing in the Workplace*

placed upon them in a male dominated society. Additionally, there is nothing wrong with wanting to accentuate one's beauty, but dressing provocatively in an attempt to get ahead in the workplace is a poor strategy and quite offensive to others. Tasteless dressing in the workplace is not just an issue among women. Many men also wear inappropriate clothing at work. One of the authors remembered a time when she was working for a large social services organization. One of her male colleagues would often come to work with extremely baggy jeans that showed his boxers and heavy sweat shirts. She recalled that many of the employees who did not know him perceived him to be uneducated, but he in fact had a Masters degree. This shows that men are judged by how they dress. As a matter of fact, they are particularly judged by their appearance during interviews where they are expected to wear clean and well-fitted suits. Pastor Hokes even said that he remembers being told in college that many employers secretly feel the quality of a man's suit when they are shaking his hand. He said that this is a tactic used to determine if the person cares enough to wear a quality suit for the interview. Moreover, he said that he was told that this is often one of the reasons why men are not chosen for the position for which they are applying. Some may think that this is a harsh business practice, but people have to understand that companies can operate, implement, and enforce whatever practices that they so choose as long as it is not discriminatory or illegal. Some may even think that passing over a person for a position because of the lack of quality of his suit is discriminatory; however companies have a right to choose their guidelines for how they want their employees to dress. Even the Bible suggests that there was a dress code for the priesthood. In Exodus 28:1-43, there were strict instructions given to construct a garment to be worn for the priesthood. The strict guidelines included a breastplate, an ornament vest or ephod, a robe, a tunic, a turban, and a sash. This demonstrates that even God has standards for one's appearance in a particular profession. Therefore, people should not make any qualms about their organization's dress code policy because it is the organization's standard. In the case of Shantel and Roger in the vignette, their

51

unprofessional clothing in their respective work settings could have been a sign of defiance and rebellion given that they were unwilling to listen to wise counsel about how their style of dress was inhibiting them. People must understand the culture in which we live. We all should abide by the adage of "dressing for success". Dressing professionally and taking care of our appearance shows organizations that we have discipline and are reliable. Most employers believe that if one takes pride in their personal care then they are likely to take as much pride in and care for the organization. On the contrary, if we are unwilling to dress professionally even when there are no strict guidelines to do so then we are sending the message that we do not care enough about the organization's needs. It may seem peculiar that employers can come to this conclusion just by how someone dresses but any CEO or other high ranked professional can attest that in order for them to have moved up in their profession, they needed to dress the part. In fact, it is almost like separating yourself and being a part of a new club. For example, on many high school sports teams, there is a freshman-sophomore team, a junior varsity team, and a varsity team. Most times the uniforms differ from team to team to distinguish the players. In addition, players cannot earn a letterman jacket until they reach the varsity level. This is part of separating oneself and being accepted into an exclusive club. The same goes for graduation robes. There is a different robe for people whom graduate from high school than there is for people whom graduate college. Moreover, there are different robes for people whom graduate with Masters degrees than those whom graduate with Doctorate degrees. Consequently, if we want to move up in our professions, we have to be willing to make adjustments in our appearance and dress accordingly. The key to this is knowing whether or not we want to actually take on the new responsibility of moving up within our companies. Pastor Hokes said that if he was counseling Chantel and Roger, he would ask them to think about whether or not they really want to advance in their careers. He said that he would ask them that because acquiring more responsibility looks appealing in theory, but we really do not know what is required of us as we progress. Thus, many choose to stay because they

*Healing in the Workplace*

not willing to mature in their appearance. Often times, maturing in one's appearance requires some mentorship from other employees whom hold higher positions. For example, Roger could have benefited from being mentored and advised on corporate attire by a manager. Many times we oppose something because we do not have enough knowledge about it to make an informed decision. In Roger's circumstance, he may not have really known that there is a way that upper management dresses in a corporate setting to set themselves apart from the other employees. Chantel, on the other hand has had ongoing mentorship from her supervisor, yet she continues to shy away from wise counsel. In her case, she needed to be notified of the company's policy about dress code even on the days when they can dress casually. Her manager and/or human resources could have helped her search these guidelines in the employee handbook. In addition, if the offense continued, disciplinary actions should have been enforced. To take it a step further, organizations need to make their dress policies clear in writing. This is notably true for start up businesses whom tend to take dress codes for granted. There needs to be clear and concise guidelines for dress, even on casual days and even if employees wear uniforms. Employees and employers alike should never dismiss dress code at work as an insignificant issue. If left unwatched and unmonitored, the organization's image can be damaged. Even further, employees whom dress inappropriately at work do not realize that they are damaging their own image and opportunities to move upward in their companies. God knows that we should be judged by our talent and skill in the workplace, but He does demand that we follow the rules that are given to us at work.

## THINGS TO PONDER ON:

- Gossip is like an infectious disease. Much like a medical disease, gossiping always has a starting point as the culprit of it spreading. Ringleaders, or people who spread gossip like to cause dissension among other colleagues while they sit back and watch it all unfold. You must ask yourself this question: "Am I the gossip ringleader?"..........Matthew 24:5

- When we gossip about others, our tongues spew poison. God says that life and death is in the power of the tongue. This means that the things that we say about others can make or break them. Most people follow the adage of "sticks and stones can break their bones but words could never hurt them". However, this is untrue. Words do hurt. The Bible says that the tongue is the only part of the body that cannot be tamed. Just think about a time when someone gossiped about you. How did you feel?.........James 3:8

- Constant joke telling and teasing others in the workplace is an example of unruly behavior. It is our duty as Christians to help these people acquire discipline by taming their rebellion. If left unaddressed by those whom are more mature in Christ, God can hold the more mature Christian accountable for the joketeller's actions......1 Thessalonians 5:14

- Have you ever thought about what makes someone a clown? Many of the people whom are office clowns are unstable and are double-minded. One minute they are quiet only because they received a reprimand and in the same moment they are loud and obnoxious. The word of God suggests that these type of people are double-minded in all areas of their lives. The sad part about these type of individuals is that their behavior can lead them to a path of destruction without them even recognizing it........James 1:8

- Many people who do not adhere to the rules of the workplace have an un-teachable spirit which results from rebellion. These type of people are rebellious because they have too much pride and do not want to humble themselves. We all can learn from

*Healing in the Workplace*

someone else's way of life yet many of us are too prideful to acknowledge that we do not have all of the answers. We must remember that God's word is true. Pride DOES come before the fall........Proverbs 29:23

- Hating instruction from those whom are in positions of power is ungodly. If we do not want to be instructed at work about things such as our appearance then we are suggesting that we hate God. We may not always agree with our employers' rules, but we have to respect the position that they hold. Besides, they are the ones whom are signing our paychecks......Proverbs 5:12-13

# LACK OF MOTIVATION FOR UPWARD MOBILITY

Anyone who has managed a team whether it is in sports or at work has been concerned about keeping their members motivated to complete tasks. Motivation at work is a complex issue because there are several things that can motivate someone. The pay, the benefits, the connection to others, the clients, or the work fulfillment can all be motivating factors that keeps people coming to work. We all can be motivated at work for different reasons, yet it continues to be an area of concern. One of the reasons why management is often concerned about employee motivation is because it is directly associated with productivity. In other words, the more employees are motivated, the more likely they are to be productive and vice versa. Essentially, the bottom line for organizations is profitability and management. Although motivation is often researched and analyzed as an organizational issue, it can also be an individual problem. We have all seen it before at work where there were a handful of employees whom we thought were "overachievers". They often stayed after work when their shift ended to complete their tasks or they volunteered to lead projects, or they even went out of their way to help their colleagues on various tasks. We often wondered about them and speculated that they were attempting to win some form of affection or kudos from the boss; or we may have thought that they

*Healing in the Workplace*

were just neurotic and did not have lives of their own. Unbeknownst to many of us, this type of behavior is actually classified as organizational citizenship. People whom display organizational citizenship tend to show up to work early or on time; help others on tasks; or go above and beyond their duties. Many researchers have even suggested that organizational citizenship contributes to a happier work environment. Although this form of behavior is classified as organizational citizenship, it can also be linked to motivation. This is not to say that if one does not score high on the organizational citizenship scale that he/she is not motivated. However, there is something to be said about how much effort one puts into a task. You see, motivation is a direct reflection of commitment. The more motivated we are to do something, the more we are willing to commit ourselves and put our entire selves into the task. God's word says a lot about commitment. In 1 Timothy 4:14-15, the Bible states that we all have been given talents that should not be neglected and that we should meditate on them and give of ourselves entirely to them. Far too often, people are unmotivated or have lack of commitment to something because they have yet to recognize the gifts and talents put before them by God. When people do not understand the gifts that God has given them, they are lost and many unwarranted spirits set in like the spirit of fear or the spirit of rebellion. These spirits stop us from achieving the goals that God has placed in our hearts. Many of us aspire for promotions to higher ranked positions or more opportunities to showcase our abilities at work, but many of us are held back by our own lack of commitment and motivation. Instead of throwing ourselves completely into accomplishing the goal, we allow these ungodly spirits to seep in and then we make excuses and blame our bosses or the organization for hindering us. God wants us to know that we are no longer held in bondage and we have become free to accomplish any and eveything that we set out to do. However, He clearly tells us in His word that we have to be motivated and committed to accomplishing our goals. Jesus is the prime example of being motivated and committed to completing a task when He died for us. He was motivated by the idea of us having eternal life in the Lord

*L'Orangerie Crawford & Terri Harrison*

and He followed through with His commitment to God and to us by dying on the cross. If Jesus could put Himself wholeheartedly into dying for our sins, then why can't we commit ourselves to accomplishing the things that we want to do?

## Scenario - THE PROCRASTINATOR:

*Tanner is a junior advertiser at Bendel and Smith Advertising. He is well liked by his colleagues and his supervisor. Tanner has not had an easy road to get to where he is at right now, but he considers himself blessed. Tanner is being chosen out of three other junior advertisers to be given an opportunity to be project manager of a mass media campaign for the company's largest client. Tanner was honored by the consideration since junior advertisers are rarely asked to be project managers. His supervisor told him that he needs to submit a strategic plan for the project and sign up to take additional training in order to be considered for the position. Tanner was initially thrilled but after reality set in, he realized that this opportunity would mean that he would have additional responsibilities in which he was not confident that he could handle. Tanner eventually puts off doing the strategic plan for the project and neglects to sign up for the training. He was given a month to prepare himself, but now has only two weeks left and still no progress. When asked by his supervisor about his progress, Tanner smiles, lies to her and tells her that he's got it under control. Fast forward, Tanner has one week left and he still has not completed his obligation. The day of submission, his supervisor comes to his desk to request for his strategic plan. Tanner, with his head hung low, tells her that he failed to do the training and did not complete the strategic plan. He saw the look of disappointment in his supervisor's eyes. She responded by saying "I don't understand this Tanner. You are one of my brightest employees. You would have surely been chosen to be project manager." All Tanner could do is just look at her while feeling a deep sadness in the pit of his stomach.*

*Healing in the Workplace*

Many of us have been plagued with the spirit of procrastination. Some people have a more serious problem with this than others. For these individuals, procrastination is so consuming that it becomes a pattern of behavior and a way of life. It has become so pathological for these individuals that it impacts almost, if not all aspects of their lives. You may see that they not only procrastinate on completing a task at work, but they may want to go back to school and they procrastinate getting the necessary information for the program in which they want to attend. You may also see them procrastinate on organizing their garage or even going to the bank to cash their checks. This pattern of behavior may seem inconsequential to most, but it is actually a hinderance to one's quality of life. Moreover, if left unattended, procrastination will begin to control our lives instead of we controlling it. There are many things that cause people to procrastinate. First, we must understand that God did not design us to be procrastinators. This behavior is something learned; primarily from our childhood and early life. Some psychologists believe that procrastination can even be a learned behavior from one's family of origin. For example, if a child sees his parents procrastinate then he is more likely to procrastinate as well and perceive this behavior as being normal. This; however is not true of all people whom grew up in families of procrastinators. Some people actually fight against their learned procrastination by being overly organized to the point of being anal. There are many forms of procrastinators including those whom wait to the last minute to complete a task to seek out a thrill from the pressure of time, those whom procrastinate to avoid something, or those whom are indecisive. People whom are thrill seekers and adrenaline junkies often have addictive personalities. They are in constant search for their next fix even at the cost of their own lives. People whom consciously procrastinate to feel the rush of the pressure of working on a task often lie to themselves by saying that they work well under pressure but the fact is that they do not understand the concept of work at all. Work is intended be comprised of well thought out and planned tasks and if we do not slow down and map out what we are suppose to do, how can we perform to the best of our abilities? These individuals were likely to wait until the last minute to complete a task and only did so because of the threat of punishment at the hands of their caregivers. Moreover, those whom procrastinate out of avoidance are crippled by fear. They are paralyzed by the fear of the unknown and possibly by the fear failing at or achieving or something. These individuals were less likely validated as children and their efforts were likely to be ignored or minimized. This, unfortunately may have contributed to their distorted belief that their efforts to do something were pointless. As adults, these distorted thought processes may have stayed with them and when faced with a challenge or obstacle, they are more likely to put off any effort because of that paralyzing fear. Conversely, many people whom procrastinate because of their indecisiveness are often afraid of their own abilities. They are afraid of their ability to make a decision and ability to stick with that decision. These people were likely to be given too many responsibilities as children and in turn often failed because they were not equipped as children to handle adult obligations; or they were likely children whom were not given any decision making power in their family, thus they grew up not trusting their own ability to make decisions. The underlying concern for these type of procrastinators is that they are often in search of something to distract them. In the spiritual sense, these type of people are runners. They tend to run from things and are often running from themselves. For instance, have you ever known someone who constantly moves around from city to city or from state to state, with the exception of being in the armed services? These type of people are major procrastinators because their constant moving acts as a distractor from accomplishing goals in their lives. They are often always in search for something but tend to never find it which is why they constantly move. People whom are chronic procrastinators have a void in their lives that needs to be filled with God's love. The double-sidedness of procrastination is that is unlikely to stop this behavior if there is a lack of motivation and commitment to do so. God wants us to know that procrastination is the behavior resulting from a lack of motivation and commitment. Far too often, people assume that just by having motivation and commitment will produce results.

*Healing in the Workplace*

However, this is false because God always instructs us to put action behind our commitment. Pastor Hokes said that procrastination never produces purpose and if we are not walking in our purpose then how can we be productive to the advancement of God's kingdom? The book of Jonah comes to mind as it relates to procrastination. In Jonah 1:1, God told Jonah to go to Nineveh for the purpose of preaching to the evildoers in that region. However, Jonah was disobedient and went to Tarshish to flee from God's presence. Jonah 1:4 says that the Lord sent out a storm at the sea because of Jonah's disobedience. The mariners were afraid but Jonah just laid down and fell asleep. The story goes on to account for the consequences for Jonah's disobedience and how he ended up still doing God's will and preaching at Nineveh. We have to know that when we procrastinate on a task, we are being disobedient to God because we are not walking in His purpose for our lives. Some people may say that moving too fast to accomplish something is also out of the will of God and though it is advantageous to plan out things beforehand, it is only true if God told us to do so. There are so many examples in the Bible of when God has told someone to complete a task, but He would either tell them to wait for guidance or just get up and do it. This is why we have to constantly have our ears turned toward Him. We have to trust in the Lord's word and know that He is not going to lead us to a place where we cannot accomplish the task. He already knows before He gives us the directive that we are well equipped for the job, but we have to trust that this is true. Pastor Hokes said that he tells people whom he counsels that when God calls us to do something, He has already qualified us. The issue is that many of us do not have the confidence in our abilities and would rather either procrastinate or avoid doing the task altogether because of our perceived incompetence. This was possibly the case for Tanner in the vignette since he was baffled at the idea of being chosen as a project manager even though he was only a junior advertiser. So many times, we lose faith in ourselves because of several reasons. Many of us were told all of our lives by others that we were unworthy, unlovable, and incapable. The sad part about this is that we had no choice in believing it because we had forgotten what God says about us. If only we could see ourselves through God's eyes, then we would know that we are more than able to accomplish our goals and we would no longer have to procrastinate. First Lady Hokes said that people have to testify to themselves and affirm that they are worthy and lovable, otherwise the enemy will torment them with low self-esteem. We also procrastinate because we haven't the slightest clue on how to set goals and stick to them. Tanner may have procrastinated on his task because he may have gone through all of his life without knowing how to set goals. One of the ways to learn how to set goals is the write down our dreams, aspirations, and visions. Pastor Hokes reminded us that God says that when we want to set a goal, we must write it down and make it plain. This helps because many people are visual learners and writing their goals down and keeping them in clear view will help them to meditate on it daily. Many people whom have difficulties with goal setting may also benefit from creating a vision board. Some of the traditional vision boards are made in poster form and places a picture of the person surrounded by images of people the person wants to become and images of things that the person wants to obtain. This may seem elementary, but it definitely serves a purpose for people whom cannot make goals for themselves. Another option that Pastor Hokes said that he uses with people is to list their priorities from 1 to 10 with the number 1 being the most important and 10 being the least important. Then he said that he likes to help people create a timeline of where they want to be in the next 3 to 5 years and they can chart the necessary milestones that they need to accomplish within this time frame. The important part about this is that when people can check off the milestones on their list as being accomplished, then they are more likely to develop greater feelings about themselves every time they complete the milestone. This would have helped Tanner with his project because he would have been more likely to feel confident in himself if he was able to achieve some of the smaller milestones that went into achieving the larger task of becoming project manager. Once more, he would have not had a reason to feel disappointed in himself even if he did not get the promotion at that time. There is a major difference in being

*Healing in the Workplace*

disappointed that we did not receive a promotion or an award on the job than being disappointed in ourselves for not going for the promotion or doing all that we could to receive the award. First Lady Hokes said that the worst feeling is to disappoint oneself. This is a feeling that is touching to the core and puts our heads further and further into the sand until we are so deep in it that we cannot come out of it. We have to understand that procrastination is a choice and not an acquired trait. We can break free from procrastination if we are willing to commit ourselves to doing the daily behaviors that will retrain us. We have to commit to encouraging ourselves daily and commit to working toward our goal no matter how tough it may seem. Besides, Pastor Hokes revealed that it is only in the face of adversity is when we get to know what we are truly made of, which is more than what we imagined as the children of the kingdom.

## FEAR OF FAILING:

*Goldenblatt, Brookes, and Schmidt is a premiere law firm in Los Angeles and has taken on some of the toughest criminal cases in Los Angeles' history and employs some of the most dynamic lawyers in the country. Needless to say, everyone in this law firm takes what they do seriously. Even the paralegals and clerks are tough. Nancy has been employed at the law firm for 5 years now. She comes from humble beginnings, growing up in Boyle Heights which is a small town on the outskirts of Los Angeles. She was taught the value of hard work by her parents who immigrated to Los Angeles from Mexico in the early 1970s. It has always been Nancy's dream to be a lawyer, ever since she was a small girl when she witnessed the injustice of how her family and friends were treated by the police just because they were immigrants. Nancy believed that taking this job as a law clerk would be the first step of learning laws and ultimately attending law school at USC. She was very happy to go to work every day, but she also felt extreme pressure because she felt as if she was carrying the weight of her neighbor on her*

63

*shoulders. Over the past 5 years, she has had opportunities to move up as a paralegal but was ambivalent out of fear of failing and letting her family and friends down. As a result, Nancy is stuck in a position that she knows is not a reflection of her worth as an employee. She has even seen three other clerks move into paralegal positions at the firm.*

Some people have a lack of motivation to move upward within their profession or organization because they have a fear of failing. They may fear failing themselves, failing others, or both. Still, this type of fear causes people to feel out of control and unhappy with themselves. These people tend to exhibit cowardice behaviors that can keep them stuck in unpleasant environments, often for the rest of their lives. The irony in this is that these type of individuals are cowards because they are desperately afraid of unpleasant or dangerous things, yet they are often already stuck in unpleasant or dangerous environments but they are too cowardly to believe God to remove them from the situation. God does understand that fear is a human response that we all have felt and will continue to feel. However, we will not be removed from our unfavorable situations and move into our personal Canaan if we allow fear to run our lives.

If you think about it, fear is all in the mind. When people are afraid of public speaking, for example, they are not really afraid of the people that they have to speak in front of. They are really more concerned about the thoughts that they have already created in their minds about what these people might say and/or think about them. Some of these negative thoughts might be "They will think that I am not articulate" or "What if they think I am boring?" These are all distorted thoughts of the mind. People whom are afraid of failing are not actually afraid of failure, but they are afraid of aftermath that can potentially occur if they fail. Furthermore, these are tricks of the enemy to attack our minds. Satan likes to enter into our thoughts and attack our minds because He knows if thoughts become infected then so can our

*Healing in the Workplace*

emotions, and then eventually our behavior. Satan is always on a mission to destroy our lives which is why we must stayed prayed up and confess God's word over our lives on a daily basis. Otherwise, we all can be weak to His devices. Consider the story of Adam and Eve. Satan successfully entered into Eve's mind by filling it with doubt and had her believing that God really did not mean that she and Adam could not eat fruit from the forbidden tree. Although Satan's tactics were cunning, Eve still had a responsibility to protect her thoughts from His manipulation. The same goes for us when we have fears; especially fear of failing that keep us from moving into our rightful positions as kingdom children. There are various reasons why people are afraid of failing at a task; particularly as it relates to work. However, you will find that this type of fear generally plays out in most areas of these people's lives. One of the reasons why people are afraid of failing is because they may have grown up in a household or experienced somewhere early on that it was unacceptable to fail. Many times, children whom grow up in households where there are perfectionists do not have permission to make mistakes and rather than attempting to complete a task, they do not engage in the task out of fear of being ridiculed if they do fail. This is not to say that all people whom have fear of failing grew up in authoritarian and perfectionist households. Some of them may have experienced this rigidity in school and it resulted in them being afraid to fail. At the other end of the spectrum, some people whom fear failure may have grown up not being allowed to make mistakes and were overly coddled by their caregivers. As parents, we must allow our children to make mistakes. Even small children need to understand the value in making mistakes. Imagine a small toddler attempting to master a task requiring motor skills. If the parent constantly steps in and does the task for him when she sees that he is struggling with it, the child never learns that it is alright to make a mistake on it and he has to keep trying. The same goes for not giving children consequences as they grow up. If children are not given consequences because of their poor behavior and are instead rewarded by either the parent ignoring the behavior or bribing the child with rewards to get her to stop misbehaving, then the child never learns that she even made a mistake in the first place. People whom grew up in these type of environments are likely to fear failure because they were not given a chance to experience what it really is. First Lady Hokes said that failure acts a learning tool to build tenacity and character. Failure helps people recognize that they are flawed and that there are people out there whom are better at certain things than they are. Knowing this helps reduce the likelihood of developing narcissistic traits. In addition, failure teaches us to persevere and problem solve. One of the greatest things that people could ever learn is to solve problems because they will learn positive coping skills and learn to trust that they can take care of themselves. Furthermore, as Christians, we should always include God as part of our problem solving plan. The issue with many parents whom reared their children without consequences or without allowing them to make mistakes is that they often wake up to their wrongdoing and try to teach them these skills when they are near adulthood. The problem with this is that we cannot turn away from a negative behavioral patterns in our children for most of their lives and expect for them to learn better skills once they become teenagers or young adults. We have to teach them these skills such as problem solving from the start so that they will not stray from this teaching as they get older. Nevertheless, as we grow into adulthood, we have the responsibility of learning these skills even if they were not taught to us as children; especially if the lack of having these skills are impeding our lives and affecting the lives of others around us. Most people whom fear failure are stuck in a "rut" and will often blame other people or other things for this. They clearly know that there is something wrong, yet they choose not to fix it. God instructs us to make a commitment to Him and to ourselves to fix our problems. Most of the time when there is a problem, it is because we have lack of information to help us get through and eventually overcome that problem. What's more, we have to be motivated to seeking out information to help us overcome our fear. In Matthew 7:7, the word says to ask and it shall be given unto you. Many people interpret this scripture as referring to material gains; however God is talking about anything that we are in

*Healing in the Workplace*

search for, even information. Once we receive this information, we have to ponder on it, process it, and make a Godly decision. In Nancy's case, she was overtaken by fear because she did not want to let her family and her neighborhood down if she had failed at her attempt of becoming a lawyer. This is a common reason why people are held back because they do not want to disappoint the people closest to them. These people were probably the "golden" children of the family and were often told that their success was their families' success. And although this is true that our success is often a reflection of the values that our parents instilled in us, there comes a time when our success should be for ourselves and for the glorification of our Father in heaven. We should never be made to feel pressure from our loved ones into living our lives for them or living out their dreams. As parents, it is our job to train our children to be the best that they can be and live out the purpose that God has for their lives. It was noble of Nancy to have wanted her loved ones to be proud of her. However, she needed to understand where her blessings, gifts, and talents come from. When we understand that God has given us the desires in our hearts and the talents to achieve those desires, then we will have tunnel vision and not allow the pressure from those around us to get to us. First, we have to know that our purpose for our lives does not come from our family and friends. They were not designed to give us the blueprint of our lives; that is God's job. The best that they can do is equip us with tools as children, intercede for us, and confirm the things that God has revealed to us in our lives. People who are afraid of failing need to find ways to break this pattern quickly. One of the things that they can start off by doing is not taking themselves too seriously. It is certainly alright to be serious when it is time to be, but letting go of inhibitions is a step toward accepting one's flaws. These people need to give themselves permission to make a simple mistake and chart down their thoughts and feelings associated to the mistake that was made. They may actually find that their thoughts were more of a distortion than a reality. They should also chart down the consequences of the mistake that they made. They may find that the consequence was not as severe as they initially thought. These type of people should also understand that the tasks that they are avoiding to complete are actually extremely important to them which is why they hold off on following through with the tasks out of fear of messing it up. These people are desperately afraid of losing or failing at something near to their hearts that they actually lose it or fail at it. It is a self-fulfilling prophecy. Once they understand the importance of these tasks in their lives, they can understand that anything that is important should be cultivated and not avoided. Also, once they gain that understanding, they can begin to make small steps toward change. It was clear that becoming a lawyer was close to Nancy's heart, but she needed to cultivate this rather than run from it. She could have started off with pursuing one or two law classes rather than immersing herself in law school if she was still hesitant. Once she completed those two classes, then she could have moved on to more classes until she received her law degree. Much like Nancy, people whom are afraid of failing are often running from their call from God. God loves that the desire that He places in our hearts is that important to us that we do not want to mess it up in anyway. However, when He calls, He does expect us to answer. The great thing about God is that when He calls us to complete a task, whether it be to change careers or apply for a new position and we continue to run from it, He still gives us mercy. In Romans 11:29, God says that the gifts and calling from Him is irrevocable. Therefore, we might as well answer to what He wants us to do from the beginning. We will be much happier that we did it His way instead of the hard way.

## FEAR OF ACHIEVING:

*Tran is a 37 year old mechanical engineer employed at a governmental transportation agency. She is hard working, cultured, and easy going. There have been talks going around the office about the agency implementing a supervisors test to help promote mechanical engineers into managerial positions. All of Tran's team members encourage her to apply for the test because she is the most qualified. She reluctantly takes the test, but does it just to please her team. Much to her surprise, she passes the test and is even offered the position to manage entry level engineers. Tran is threatened by her new found status and constantly tells herself that she is doing a horrible job, is unqualified, does not understand why she was chosen, and no one likes her because she is foreign. On the contrary, Tran is doing an exceptional job as a supervisor, everyone is thrilled to work for her, and no one cares about her being foreign. This is not the first time that the "negative tape recorder" has played in Tran's head about her abilities. She has always compared herself to her older sister, Li, a surgeon in the Boston area. Tran's fear of success has even played out in her personal relationships in which she has turned down a marriage proposal from a smart, handsome, and hard-working man who adores her. Her fear of achieving has been a constant set back in her life and she just can't seem to shake the negative thoughts about herself. One day, Tran's "negative tape recorder" became overwhelming and she resigned from her position as a supervisor one month before her probationary period ended. She even requested to return to her previous position as a mechanical engineer.*

Most people believe that the fear of success is a fabricated concept since almost all of us desire some form of success in our lives. The reality is that many people do fear success and will sabotage themselves so that they will not have to face that fear. Unlike the fear of failure, the fear of achieving holds a stigma because it suggests that people whom have this fear somehow want to be losers in life. This could not be further from the truth. People whom experience this fear have the same dreams and aspirations as anyone else. The dreams and aspirations are less likely to be fearful, but the idea of change entering one's life as a result of success is what is quite possibly paralyzing these type of individuals. God needs these individuals to understand that embracing change is a part of life. No one progresses to any point in life without change happening.

Change is an interesting and complex concept because it is multidimensional. It refers to a shift in something, it invokes fear because there is an element of not knowing, and it takes us out of our comfort zone. Many people lack the motivation to move upward within the workplace because they fear the changes that it might bring to themselves and others around them. shifting things in one's life requires a discipline that many people do not have. Think of going back to college after 15 years of working. This will require the shifting of many things in one's life. Perhaps there will no longer be room to hang out with friends on a weekly basis because time is needed to complete homework assignments; or perhaps there will be less time to play basketball at the gym after work because classes are in session during this time. These are examples of change creating a shift in one's life. The problem with people whom fear success is that the idea of achieving the success is appealing, but the shift in their lives is not. A shift in one's life requires a sacrifice that these type of people are typically not willing or are afraid to make. Also, the fear of not knowing what is up a head is very serious because it is often based on fantasy rather than on reality. With the example of going back to school, perhaps one speculated that he could continue to hang around his friends and play basketball at the gym all while going to school, but realized that this was unlikely. This is not to say that people have to give up their lives entirely when making major changes in their lives, but it does require a great deal of delaying gratification and moving some things around to reach the overall goal. Additionally, these shifts in our lives as a result of change can make us uncomfortable because they are designed to stretch us and help us grow. Going back to the example of going back to school after 15 years, it will undoubtedly take someone out of her comfort zone because she has not been used to writing papers and sitting in front of a professor for quite some time. That uncomfortable feeling is actually normal and signals to us that we are in fact growing. Case in point, people do not call the pain from our bodies distending during adolescence as growing pains for nothing. People whom fear success often fear the unnerving feelings that come along with the success. Many of these people are afraid that

*Healing in the Workplace*

they will have to leave certain people behind if they are not in accordance with their purpose or they may even fear having to leave old and unhealthy lifestyle choices behind. Additionally, they may fear that Having to do this may cause them to feel lonely. However, if they are around people whom do not enhance to their purpose then they are already lonely. If we are following in God's special purpose for our lives, we may have to limit our contact with our families whom are living ungodly or we may have to leave those friends whom constantly bring trouble in our lives. God understands that this is not an easy thing to do and in fact, it may be one of the hardest things to do. However, it may have to be done in order to fulfill His will. In addition, it requires a deeper level of maturity to be able to stand alone for the purpose of obtaining the success that God has for us. Many of these people have difficulties in maturing because they fear the responsibility that comes along with success. God clearly states to us that when much is given, much is required. God loves and believes in us so much that He requires that we have responsibilities to help us grow. Yet many of these individuals look at the responsibilities that come along with success as a burden. They do not see it as them moving forward and advancing in life. In 1 Corinthians 13:11, the word says that as children, we speak as children, but as we grow, we are to put away childish things. There are several explanations for people fearing success. One of the reasons is that they often believe that somehow they do not deserve the success. This goes back to the distorted thinking that happens when we allow the enemy to enter into our minds and attack our thoughts. We may feel that we are not special enough, or smart enough to acquire success. In a work setting, we may even believe that someone better may deserve that promotion that we received. This type of thinking is a strong indicator of having low self-esteem. Pastor Hokes said that people whom think this way are in a battlefield of the mind and often do not love themselves. Many people whom have these distorted thoughts about themselves and their abilities were likely to grow up feeling unloved by significant people in their lives. No matter how well they did in school, how well mannered they were, or how big of a heart they had; they were less likely to receive validation from the most important people in their lives as children. Parents have to balance giving their children consequences and constructive feedback with validating them and telling them how wonderful they are. God is the ultimate example of loving us and telling us how worthy we are of His love but still chastising us if we do wrong. Another reason that people fear achievement is because they believe that the feat is impossible. Many people stop themselves from going for managerial positions because they are looking at the color of their skin as a barrier or believe that they will not get hired because of their lack of education. God wants all of His children to know that all things are possible through Him. In fact, one of the authors recalled a time when she was unemployed for several years and in dire need of a job. She initially thought that not working for that length of time would have disqualified her from a position in which she was interested. She; however saw God show up and show out because He gave her favor with the hiring manager and she got the job. In Acts 10:34, Peter tells Cornelius, the gentile that God is no respecter of person. This means that He shows no favoritism and if He can make a way for the author, then He can make a way for any one of us in our lives. Many people are afraid of accomplishing things because they are distrustful of their abilities. They often have an "I can't" attitude that has been quite possibly stifling them their entire lives. Often times, these individuals have this type of mindset because they are comparing themselves to others. For instance, Tran in the vignette was and has possibly comparing herself to her older sister since they were children. Looking at someone else's achievements and believing that the grass is greener on the other side will always cause us to look at the negatives in our lives. There will always be someone smarter and more talented than us. However, God designed us to be unique from others. Pastor and First Lady Hokes both said that these type of individuals have to see themselves the way God sees them. In addition, Pastor Hokes said that God will never help us be someone else but He will help us be the best that we can be. Moreover, some people whom fear success do not want to deal with the feelings of guilt. This is also an issue in survivor's guilt

*Healing in the Workplace*

because people believe that they have done something wrong by surviving a horrendous event. Tran and others like her may have been suffering from the guilt of making it into a higher ranked position while leaving their colleagues behind. Though this is comprehensible, it can set people back because they are not living their lives for themselves. Pastor Hokes said that people have to set their own goals and live out their own aspirations and not feel guilty for the blessings that God has given them. There are some simple steps that people can make to help them cope with this particular issue. They can first start off by accepting and acknowledging their gifts and talents. God wants us to stop being ashamed of the great things He has done for us. In fact, we are poor witnesses when we minimize God's blessings in our lives. The next thing that we can do is surround ourselves with positive thinking people. It is amazing how being around negative people can cause us to feel negative as well. People whom are negative in their thoughts and whom live a negative lifestyle are like sponges and will soak up every ounce of one's energy. It is best to be around others whom are doing positive things in their lives and are truly living a Godly life and not just going through the motions of Christianity. Many Christians are in bondage because they are living unholy and think that going to church every Sunday is suffice. However, many Christians with negative lifestyles do not have a relationship with Christ. Once we surround ourselves with positive people, we will begin to think positively of ourselves. One other thing that we can do to combat the fear of success is to challenge ourselves to volunteer to work with others on or even head projects at work. This will take us out of our comfort zone, but it will also help us from being withdrawn. Pastor Hokes suggested that managers whom have employees that are fearful of achievement should praise them for achieving tasks as often as they can. Once these employees feel that they are a valuable part of the team and/or organization, they will begin to have less fears of achieving tasks at work. We all have fears and God knows this because He created us. However, God knows that through Him we can conquer those fears, but only if we allow Him to move in our lives.

*L'Orangerie Crawford & Terri Harrison*

## THINGS TO PONDER ON:

- Oftentimes, we say that we will do things tomorrow but we do not realize how cocky and self- righteous that statement is. The truth is that tomorrow is not promised to any one of us. We must always keep in mind that the Lord did not put off things that needed immediate attention until tomorrow. In the book of James, we are admonished: "Come now, you who say, Today or tomorrow we will go to such and such a city, spend a year there, buy and sell, and make a profit whereas you do not know what will happen tomorrow. For what is your life? It is even a vapor that appears for a little time and then vanishes away".......... James 4:13-14

- Who cares? It can wait! Later! At some point, we all have said this but end up paying the price for procrastinating. Delay is the beginning stage of procrastination; procrastination is a present and future killer! God respects time which is why He does things descent and in order. In the book of Matthew, He is clear about leaving tomorrow for tomorrow: "Therefore do not worry about tomorrow, for tomorrow will worry about its own things. Sufficient for the day is its own trouble"........Matthew 6:14

- Stagnation is a form of fear. Staying in one place too long usually means that one is afraid to move on to the next phase of life. We start believing and telling ourselves "we do not have the skills that it takes to perform the job". Simply put, fear of failing is sabotage to one's life! The Lord commands that we do not walk in the spirit of fear but in power, love and soundness of mind "For God has not given us the spirit of fear, but of power and of love and of a sound mind"........2 Timothy 1:7

- Listening requires an action! Just as listening requires action; so does fear of failing. Fear of failing is a choice in which place

*Healing in the Workplace*

limitations on ourselves. The Lord paid the ultimate price for our success on Calvary with the shedding of his blood. We have a promise from Him that we can succeed. It's time to stand up and be accountable for our actions; "Have I not commanded you? Be strong and of good courage: do not be afraid, nor be dismayed for the Lord your God is with you wherever you go.......Joshua 1:9

- It is never a good idea to measure our gifts, talents and abilities to that of others. No two people are alike. Each person is unique and should be treated as such. Consider Galatians 6:4-5 which states: "But let each one examine his own work, and then he will have rejoicing in himself alone, and not in another. For each one shall bear his own load."

- The importance of remembering greatness or successes in small things creates a pattern for realistic achievements. There is nothing wrong with having some apprehension about moving on to the next level. However, do not allow the fear to block the things that God has planned for your future. In order to reach your goals, you have to work in concert with the Lord. The prophet Jeremiah reminds us "For I know the thoughts that I think towards you, says the Lord, thoughts of peace and not of evil, to give you a future and a hope.........Jeremiah 29:11

# NEPOTISM

In a perfect world, the most qualified and productive employees will be hired and/or promoted in the workplace. However, many of us can attest that this is not always the case. Most companies practice nepotism or the favoring of relatives over other employees. In addition to this, many people do not equate favoritism for employees regardless of kinship as nepotism. For the purpose of this chapter, the term nepotism will be referred to as not only the favoring of family members but of other employees as well. In today's society, companies have strived to employ practices such as Affirmative Action to ensure that opportunities are given to all employees regardless of race, creed, or sexual orientation. The issue of fairness is the underlying concern as it relates to nepotism. In addition to such fair practices as Affirmative Action, many companies have established and enforced anti-nepotism policies such as forbidding the hiring of relatives to make certain that employees are working in a fair and just environment. Other companies are not as stringent with their policies and may allow the hiring of relatives or friends but prohibit a direct working relationship between them as precautionary measures. Regardless of where a company stands on their anti-nepotism policies, they must understand the potential dangers of nepotism and devise strategies to help decrease and/or prevent such dangers. Some of the immediate dangers of nepotism, if done unprofessionally is the loss of employee morale. Many employees will begin to feel a disconnect with the organization if they believe that nepotism is obstructing their opportunities to move up within the organization. Furthermore, they

*Healing in the Workplace*

may begin to feel devalued and start to lose interest in their work duties. Another danger of nepotism is the risk of lawsuits. Many employees may believe that they are being discriminated against if they fail to be promoted while a relative or favorite employee of a manager is promoted instead. The fact still remains that nepotism is an issue that is not going away; especially since many companies do not have anti-nepotism procedures in place. Once more, it has been a matter that dates back to Biblical times. For instance, In Genesis 47:11-12, Joseph appointed his father and brothers positions in the land of Egypt and provided them with the goods of the land. In addition, 1 Samuel 14:50 states that the commander of Saul's army was Abner, the son of Ner who was Saul's uncle. These are just a few of the examples of nepotism in the Bible. The concern for most employees is not that nepotism is actually happening since many of us can be honest in saying that they would look out for their relatives or friends if they needed a job. However, the real issue for employees is that it is often done unprofessionally where the most qualified and suitable employees are overlooked for lesser qualified employees just because they are related to or are friends with a decision maker in the organization. God is for protecting and looking out for our loved ones whether it be telling them about an open position at our company or informing them of an upcoming training course to improve upon their skills. However, God is against edifying loved ones while treating other employees poorly.

## Scenario - KINSHIP:

*Imagine that you hold a senior executive position at a reputable company and you supervisor several departments in this company. Under your direction are very capable and intelligent employees whom significantly contribute to your managerial success. Additionally, many of these employees are equipped with exceptional skills and have college degrees that would help them have their own managerial success someday. Your daughter works in another department at the same company and you have had no contribution to her employment at this company. By all intents and purposes, your daughter is a competent worker and a valuable employee. One of your employees has left the company to go back to school and you are in a company- wide search to fill the position. You soon learn that your daughter is having marital problems in which her husband is considering leaving her and she is faced with supporting her two small children and paying a mortgage on her own. Your daughter's current salary does not support the lifestyle of a single parent and you do not want her and your grandchildren to live uncomfortably. If she were to acquire this new position in your department, her salary would increase exponentially. Do you think that hiring your daughter would cause an uproar amongst the other employees? Do you think that it would be justifiable to hire your daughter? If given the opportunity, would you establish other solutions to help your daughter?*

There are several things for one to consider when hiring his/her children in the organization. First, one has to consider if their children are equipped with the skills to handle the position for which they are hired. Once more, it is important to consider the feelings of other employees and how the hiring of one's children would disrupt the environment. Genesis 25:27 affirms that Isaac and Rebekah had two sons, Jacob and Esau. Jacob was mild mannered while Esau was a skilled hunter and a man of the field. In Genesis 27:1-4, Isaac grew old and asked Esau to hunt food for him to cook before he died and he would receive Isaac's blessing. This suggests that Isaac knew that Esau was more skilled than Jacob to fetch him food in his old age. Just like Isaac, we have to carefully deliberate on our children's skills before we hire them for any position in our company. Furthermore, the story of David and Saul in the Bible points out how employees might feel if we hire our children in our organization. Saul was simply jealous of David because he was next in line as King. Saul even went to great lengths to have David killed because of his jealousy. Many employees may not understand why a manager might hire their children nor are they likely to care. They may

*Healing in the Workplace*

develop envy or even hatred toward the manager and the child because of this. Though these feelings are ungodly, managers must be prepared to deal with such consequences if they do decide to hire their children for a job. Moreover, managers must always keep the organization's best interest in mind. Therefore, it may be in the organization's best interest to hire one's child if he/she is skilled, hardworking, and knowledgeable about the position. However, if the child is none of those things then their employment would probably be more of a detriment to the organization. Additionally, managers whom are considering hiring their children should never give them preferential treatment over other employees. Think about Donald Trump and his philosophy on hiring his children for his company. He has made it clear that his children are well educated in and knowledgeable about their field and he would have no qualms in firing them if they began to be unproductive. Pastor Hokes said that parents can learn a lot from Trump's attitude toward his children. He said that it is important to teach our children the value of hard-work and not to just rely on their parents to give them everything. Pastor Hokes even recalled going to work with his father and watching how hard he worked. He said that his father would always implant little nuggets of wisdom on how to get a job and keep a job. He remembered his father telling him that if he finds a job that does not wake him up in the morning then he does not need that job. In other words, he said that his father meant that we all have to be inspired by what we do knowing that it is our ministry rather than just getting up and going to work to collect a paycheck. First Lady Hokes said that parents need to give their children teachable moments about the workplace and the value of hard work. She said that the word of God says that parents need to give their children discipline and correction (Proverbs 22:15). Discipline does not only refer to punishment but it also means giving them structure, guidance, and training them to be diligent employees. First lady Hokes also said that parents have a responsibility to train their children to achieve things for themselves even if they work for their parents. This way, they will learn the necessary tools to be able to step out on their own one day. Once more, they will be better prepared at making wise decisions for their career path. Pastor Hokes said that if he was the parent in the vignette and was faced with the decision of hiring his daughter, he would let her know about the position and give her the option of applying. He also said that he would be fair by informing the other employees about the position. Furthermore, Pastor Hokes said that he would allow his daughter to go through the appropriate hiring process and proper protocol than simply hiring her without giving her an interview. In addition, parents have to be mindful of employee backlash and prepare their children if they decide to hire them. This would entail talking to employees about the plan to hire one's child because him or her is skilled and would bring value to the team and not because of a relational bond. Once more, parents have to talk to their children and discuss their responsibilities and state expectations for the task. Furthermore, it should be made clear that they will be treated the same as other employees even if that means that they will be written up for wrongdoings or terminated from the position. Another helpful tip when hiring children in your organization is to create team building activities so that the employees can get to know one another. This may help decrease any misperceptions or judgments that they may have had about your child. Once more, give your child an opportunity to showcase his or her talents and skills by giving them specific duties. This would help the other employees take notice of your child's aptitude and better understand your reasoning behind hiring him or her. There are several advantages and disadvantages to hire children or relatives for your organization. The decision to hire them can be catastrophic if they are unskilled and/or unwilling to prove themselves. However, they can be an asset if they are charismatic and productive employees. Managers need to be prayerful about their decision and ultimately do what is right for everyone involved.

*Healing in the Workplace*

## Scenario - SPOUSAL SUPPORT:

*Carlos and Mary have been married for 15 years and both are educators at an inner city high school in their town. Mary is an assistant principal and is head over the special education department in which Carlos teaches. One of her duties is to meet with the principal of the high school and go over school budgets. She often reports to the principal that the special education department is in dire need of a larger budget to acquire the necessary resources needed to help the students with special needs. Mary frequently advocates for her husband to attend additional trainings to be paid for by the school since he is in the process of finishing classes to obtain his special education credential. Also, she frequently assigns Carlos to lead on many of the department's projects. Kelly, a young and energetic special education teacher has taken notice of Mary's special treatment towards Carlos. She eventually confronts Mary about this. Mary was defensive and even eluded to Kelly's questioning her as insubordination. Should Kelly have confronted Mary about this issue? Does Mary have the right to give Carlos special treatment as his wife and since she is the head of the department?*

Much like hiring children for an organization, working with a spouse can have its benefits and challenges. One of the benefits of working with a spouse is building a stronger bond because of the understanding of what the other is experiencing on a daily basis. However, one of the challenges is balancing professional and personal life. This not only means ensuring that the marital bond stays intact, but that the couple does not show favoritism toward one another at the expense of the other employees. This is particularly essential if one member of the couple is the boss. Surely, it is acceptable and even expected that spouses whom work together will safeguard one another. However, it must be done in a decent and orderly fashion. When done properly, couples working together can be a blessing to both people. An example of this is Moses and his wife Zipporah. In the Old Testament of the Bible, the word shows how Zipporah and her family were of great assistance to Moses' ministry. The passages in Exodus also discusses the many challenges that they had with working together but how they overcame those challenges.

The best way to overcome the hurdles that come along with working together as a couple is to maintain open and honest communication with one another while establishing and upholding professional boundaries. It is natural for a husband and wife to watch over one another if they work together. The other employees should be aware of this fact. However, couples whom work together must always be cognizant that others may disapprove and feel uncomfortable about their working together. This means that they should not be blatant or obvious with their favoritism toward one another. First Lady Hokes said that she believes that many employees can ignore a couple's preference for one another if the couple is professional about it. For example, she said that couples never should be huddled up in one spot and talking in a conspicuous manner. This would automatically catch the attention of the other employees and they will start to believe that the couple is conspiring against the organization. It would benefit the couple to talk about job related issues at home or in a private area. Nevertheless, this is not an easy task when one of the spouses is the supervisory of the other. In this situation, it may be a time when the supervisor has to discuss job related matters with his or her spouse that may catch the eye of the other employees. This is simply an unavoidable issue. However, as a supervisor, one must be prepared for this. Pastor Hokes said that leaders always have to deal with controversy. He said that Mary in the vignette would be a poor leader if she did not prepare herself for any criticism from her employees. Many employees may believe that the other spouse is only moving up or receiving perks because he/she is married to the boss. Furthermore, some employees may be so concerned that they are tempted to confront the boss, much like Kelly did in the vignette. Though this may seem like a good idea at the time, there has to be a good amount of prayer and thought behind confronting one's

*Healing in the Workplace*

boss; especially about how he/she is running their team or department. Pastor Hokes suggested that employees should choose their battles wisely and think about the possible outcomes before confronting a supervisor about concerns. Once more, they should always be respectful in their approach. Ecclesiastes 10:4 suggests that when the spirit of the ruler comes against us, we should not lose our composure because a respectful approach can pacify a great offense. In other words, if we want to confront our bosses about an issue then we should do it calmly even if our bosses are angry. Even further, we should always be sure that we have all of the facts when confronting our bosses. In Kelly's case, she confronted Mary because of her concern of a perceived preferential treatment toward Mary's husband Carlos. Though Kelly had every right to be concerned, she may not have known all of the facts about Carlos' abilities as an employee and may have just assumed that he was being favored because of his ties to Mary. First Lady Hokes said that we have to be careful when we are questioning authority's decisions. She; however did not suggest that we should never question an authority figure, but we should do it when we have all of the facts. Kelly may not have known that Carlos was going to training so that he could receive his teaching credential and just assumed that he was being chosen by Mary because he is her husband. Furthermore, Kelly's failure to compile all of her facts before confronting Mary may have been the reason why Mary became so defensive rather than Mary becoming defensive because Kelly questioned her. Pastor Hokes recommended that we are sincere in our approach when confronting managers and not be accusatory. If our supervisors are doing something that we do not like, we must approach them with the intention of appropriately resolving the issue even if that means that we do not get what we want at that time. Instead, resolving the issue could simply mean that the supervisor takes our requests into consideration and find better ways to manage the entire team and not just one individual team member. In addition to this, spouses have to devise positive solutions when working together. They have to first know if it is the right thing for them and their relationship. They have to also treat one another with respect and

83

be a good example in the workplace. This means that they should not undermine one another's authority in front of others. An example of this is initially cutting one another off when speaking. They should also avoid competing against one another for projects or assignments. If couples can respect one another while coexisting in a work setting, there will be very few challenges that occur. For example, Pastor and First Lady Hokes reportedly have been working together in their ministry for over 30 years. They both agreed that working together as a couple has its challenges, but the rewards far outweigh the challenges; especially if one partner supports the other's vision. However, when working together is no longer working, it may be time to consider one or both partners leaving the job for another one. The best thing to do is to put the relationship first rather than to sacrifice the marital commitment over a job.

## Scenario - *FAVORED EMPLOYEE:*

*Shelly is a clinical psychology intern at a therapy clinic working with Autistic children. She has a Doctorate degree and is working toward her license as a clinical psychologist. She is working on a team with other therapists whom have Masters degrees and are also working towards their licenses. Dr. Carter has been working the field for over 25 years and is their supervisor. He often considers Shelly to be more educated than the other therapists because she has a higher degree. He tends to show her favor by sending her to trainings without sending her team members. Tamara, is one of Shelly's team members and decides to confidentially speak to Dr. Carter but does not mention Shelly's name nor does she mention any of the other team members. Instead, Tamara expresses how much she values Dr. Carter's expertise and the position that he holds, and mentions that she would like to be considered for additional training to develop her skill set. Impressed by Tamara's ambition and her approach, Dr. Carter grants her request and signs her up for the upcoming training on Behavior Analysis.*

*Healing in the Workplace*

Fraternization is another concern in the workplace because it can have negative implications for organizations. The term refers to the act of favoring people whom are nonrelatives and attempting to form a familial bond with them. There are some organizations that have policies against fraternization; however many do not. Some of the ways that people engage in fraternization in the workplace is forming romantic relationships with colleagues, calling one another cousins or siblings, or engaging in business endeavors outside of the work setting. Some of the negative consequences of such behavior is the undermining of authority and low morale. Supervisors in particular must stay clear from fraternizing with their subordinates because it can and does often lead to the disrespect of the supervisor's position at the hands of their employees. Managers whom befriend or give preferential treatment to certain employees are in a dangerous position because this behavior can gravely impact their relationship with the other employees. Jesus' management over the twelve disciples is the perfect example of how to treat employees. Jesus loved all of the disciples and chose them based on their individual characteristics. He may have known when and who to turn to depending upon the task; however He delegated responsibilities accordingly and He had a special relationship with each and every one of them.

We know that things of the world are often unfair. There will be employees whom are promoted when we believe that they do not deserve it. There will be times when our colleagues move on to work for more prestigious organizations and "leave us behind". This is all part of the working world and we have to deal with it. Even favoritism among employees may seem unfair, but it is a reality. Since we know that it occurs on a daily basis, how do we cope with it? The first thing to understand is that this type of behavior is manipulative at the hands of supervisors and employees. Some supervisors gravitate toward employees because they know that their managerial decisions will not be challenged by them or they may even prefer certain employees over others because they remind them of someone in their personal lives.

Whatever the reason, supervisors whom favor some employees over others are being ineffective leaders. Employees, on the other hand, whom monopolize their supervisors' time may be seeking out validation from them or maybe manipulating them to move up in the organization. Regardless of the explanation, these type of employees are disingenuous. The next thing to understand is that we all have a responsibility in decreasing favoritism in the workplace. Supervisors have a responsibility in being aware of how much or how little they engage with certain employees, while employees have a responsibility to be fair and not compete with one another for supervisors' time. Furthermore, people have to care about the best interest of the team and not always think of themselves. For example, there were several people in the vignette that were thinking about their best interest and disregarded the team. Shelly, the favored employee had no control over how Dr. Carter treated her. She could not help that he trusted her more than her colleagues because of her educational level. Once more, it can be safe to say that she felt good about herself after receiving validation from Dr. Carter. However, she had a responsibility to refocus the energy away from her and help showcase the talents of her team members. God says that when we are blessed and highly favored, it is our duty to give the same to others. 1 Thessalonians 5:11 says that we have to comfort one another and build each other up. This does not just refer to when we are down and out. It also refers to building each other up when we notice that others around us are not receiving the credit that they deserve. Shelly could have edified her colleagues by informing Dr. Carter that she heard about a training that would benefit the entire team and not just herself. This would have helped Shelly appear less selfish to her colleagues. Dr. Carter also had a responsibility to be objective when choosing who to send to trainings. He should have informed all of his employees about the training and allowed them to sign up for the trainings if they were interested. Furthermore, to help eliminate biases, he could have made it mandatory for the entire team to go to trainings. Once more, he should have been more selective by choosing the employees for trainings based on their need rather than on their educational level. Tamara also had a responsibility in this situation. She was very professional in her approach toward Dr. Carter. In fact, she did the right thing by expressing her respect for his position as the supervisor. First Lady Hokes said that we should always respect our supervisors' position even if we do not like or respect them personally. This means that we have to remain respectful in our tone toward them and not undermine them with others by suggesting that they are incompetent even if we sincerely believe this about them. God's will, according to 1 Peter 2:13-15 is that we honor and submit ourselves to every ordinance of man for the Lord's sake. Even if we disagree with them, we have to honor their appointed position. Tamara may not have agreed with Dr. Carter's initial decision to send Shelly on all of the trainings, but she respected him enough to approach him in a professional manner. She; however did not respect her team by letting them know that she was going to speak to Dr. Carter about training. It would have been better for her to tell her team that she has noticed that Dr. Carter only sends Shelly to the trainings and that she would like to address this with him. She could have encouraged them to also speak to Dr. Carter about this if they wanted to. That way, if the team later heard about her speaking to him, they would have not been surprised and would have less likely felt angry about it. Pastor Hokes said that he believes that Tamara was being manipulative in her actions because she was not looking out for her team. He acknowledged that it was her right to look out for herself, but he said that she needed to remember the concept of a team environment. He said that the purpose of a team is that there a collective of individuals that come together for the betterment of the team and not to advance personal agendas. One of the authors thought about a time when she was in school and learned of some information that would not only help her but would also benefit her classmates. She remembered being ill-advised to keep it to herself rather than to disclose it to them out of fear that she would lose the opportunity. However, the author reminded herself that her blessings were from God and that no man would be able to close the door on the opportunities that He ordained for her. Furthermore, she knew that she could not live with herself knowing that she purposefully withheld something good from her classmates. Consequently, she told them about the opportunity and they were grateful to her. Pastor Hokes said that whether or not we like it, we are our brother's keeper and we cannot call ourselves friends, a team, or loved ones if we are denying each other opportunities because of jealousy or competition. Besides, God's word tells us that there is more than enough room in His kingdom for His children.

## THINGS TO PONDER ON:

- One of the closest relationships is kinship. When God created us, He had one goal in mind which was to have a blood covenant relationship with man. This type of bond is the example of an earthly relationship between family which is why The Lord loves the institution of family. Should a parent always step in to help their children? The word of God says a parent should come to the aid of their children...............I Thessalonians 2:9

- Unity that is manifested in relationship is the conduit to having a connection to someone. When thinking about the strength of a healthy kinship, it can be mind blowing. Perhaps, it is sometimes hard to even imagine the magnitude of how awesome it is to be tied to another person through a blood covenant. For this purpose a parent never stops reaching out to their children. God expects parents to be there for their children and help mold them into Godly people.......I Peter 4:8

- The marital bond is the closest kinship bond. God expects married people to leave their families and create their own families with their partners. Such a bond is cherished by God in which He says that no one is to devise evil plans to separate nor drive a wedge between a marital union.......Matthew 19:6

*Healing in the Workplace*

- There are great examples of power couples working together: Brad Pitt and Angelina Jolie, Desi Arnaz and Lucille Ball, and Barack and Michelle Obama. These couples have one thing in common: their ability to stand united while working together. They are highly regarded by world standards for their outward affection towards one another and mutual respect. In the Bible, King Titus admonishes that husbands and wives are to support one another, speak good of others, and show humility......... Titus 3:2

- Job performance is rewarded in different ways such as performance appraisal, specialized training for upward mobility, and promotion. However, too many times supervisors do a poor job in measuring job performance because they do not measure employee performances equally. Showing favoritism to an employee can have damaging effects, yet God allows Christians to have favor with others in the workplace. Although God allows His children to be favored, He also wants our performances to be measured fairly and objectively........Romans 4:4

- Are you so desperate to move up in the company that you are willing to stab your coworkers in the back? Do you plot against others in the company to get ahead? Are your motives pure? How do you want others to remember you? What do you think your supervisor says about you? If you are receiving favoritism from your supervisor, does it affect your relationship with other staff? Can you be honest with yourself about these questions? Can you live up to Godly expectations of conducting yourself honorably?......I Peter 2:12

# LEADERSHIP

Leadership is a very important status; especially in the workplace. In fact, leadership is a natural part of society. Think about the many different ethnic tribes in the world. Customs and practices may be different from tribe to tribe, but the one common thread is that there is a clear leader to guide the other members. Some people are natural-born leaders and assert their way into a leadership position while others are appointed. Regardless of how one comes into his or her own as a leader, the role is often difficult. Since the responsibility of leaders are often daunting, it is important for them to have effective training to give them the tools to lead appropriately. One of the most important things that leaders must be trained on is ethics. Ethics is a word that many of us have heard at least once, but some do not have a full understanding of it. Ethics refers to the morals that governs conduct. Some people may call it their "conscious" that is guiding them in conducting in a fair and just manner, while others may call it their "little voice" inside of their head telling them to do the right thing. For we Christians, the Holy Spirit has the executive control over our lives. The Holy Spirit is the governing body that gives us discernment and helps us make wise decisions. Unfortunately for the working world, many leaders do not have ethics and repeatedly behave immorally. Consider the many examples of corporate leaders whom have swindled their clients out of billions of dollars. This behavior is not only unethical but illegal. Far too often, these type of leaders do not realize or perhaps do not care to realize that their behavior sets the tone for their employees. Whatever the leader

*Healing in the Workplace*

values, he or she will informally communicate this to employees and then the employees will begin to value these things as well. For example, if a leader highly values money, he or she will communicate this to employees by emphasizing productivity and profitability and then the employees will begin to value these things. This is not necessarily a negative thing in and of itself; however leaders must be aware of the influence that they have over others. If they are a positive influence, then their employees are likely to behave in positive ways. However, if they are negative influences, then their employees are likely to behave negatively. Think about times when we tell our children to stay away from children whom frequently misbehave or do not respect authority. We tell our children this because we understand the power of influence and we understand that children are highly impressionable. Though children can be susceptible to harmful influences, if we properly train them then we can rest easily in knowing that they will stay true to their morals and values. Just as children have a responsibility to uphold their morals even when they are pressured or negatively enticed by peers, employees also have a responsibility to maintain their morals even when their leaders are unethical. An example of this in the Bible is when King Darius decreed against prayer according to the Medes and Persian laws. Daniel stayed true to his values and was caught praying and thrown into the lion's den as a consequence. Daniel was covered by God's mercy while in the lion's den and was not harmed. When the King saw this, he ordered Daniel to be raised from the den and the King decreed that all of the kingdom must reverence God. This example is not suggesting that employees should defy their leaders. The real lesson is that when employees stay true to their morals; especially as Christians and not behave immorally even when their leaders are misguided, they may receive backlash, but God still gives His mercy and people have no choice but to acknowledge His lordship. Moreover, God expects leaders to manage with integrity. When leaders rule with integrity, it creates a stable environment for employees. Employees will feel as if they can trust the leader. However, when leaders do not have integrity, they create an unstable environment where the employees are distrustful of them

*L'Orangerie Crawford & Terri Harrison*

and are in constant fear. Additionally, because leaders have the power to impact their employees and their environment, it is highly important that they are in constant prayer and guidance from the Holy Spirit to ensure that their wisdom inspires others around them.

## Scenario - *TRANSFORMATIONAL VS. TRANSACTIONAL:*

*Rudy has just completed the trainee program at a pharmaceutical sales company in the Bay area of California. He was excited about this opportunity and eager to be a first line sales representative. While in training, he learned of the two managers of the most successful teams in the company. Douglas has the second most productive team while Katherine has had the most productive team in terms of sales for the past two years. Many of the new trainees were keen on Katherine because of her success in productivity. They heard that she is a "no-nonsense" person but were okay with this because they wanted to be part of a winning team. Douglas' team on the other hand, comes second to Katherine's team every quarter. However, Douglas manages his team quite differently than she does. He takes the time to get to know the strengths and weaknesses of his employees and he also motivates them by empowering them to try a little bit harder than they had previously done before. He always seems to know what to say and when to say it to motivate his team. Katherine's style and approach to managing her team is all about the numbers. She is very task oriented and is highly organized. She rarely empowers her employees to better their skills yet she always seems to manage to come out on top. Rudy has been grappling with deciding which team he should join, but for his fellow trainees, there is no question that Katherine is their leader. After thoughtful deliberation, Rudy chooses to join Douglas' team. After 3 months on the job, he ran into one of his fellow trainees, who is now under the management of Katherine and she told him that all Katherine cares about is meeting quotas and deadlines. She even told him that Katherine makes them work on weekends if they have not met their quotas. Rudy smiled and thought to himself that he made the right decision because Douglas has already started to groom him for a middle management position after recognizing his innate leadership ability.*

The terms transactional and transformational have been extensively researched in the business world. The two terms alludes to the differences in leadership styles. Transactional leaders are likely to motivate their employees with rewards and punishment. In addition, these type of leaders tend to be highly organized, detail oriented, and utilize their power to get their employees to complete tasks. On the other hand, transformational leaders tend to give individual attention to employees and use their role to inspire and empower employees to work beyond their duties. There has been an ongoing debate in organizational literature about which style of leadership is more effective. Some academics believe that transactional leaders get the most from their employees while other academics believe that transformational leadership brings out the most productivity. The truth is that neither of these leadership styles are right or wrong. In fact, these styles may be attributed to personality. People tend to lead according to their personalities and how they view the world. Someone who is a "Type A" personality or someone who is time-conscious and high achieving is likely to have a transactional leadership style. Transformational leaders, in contrast tend to have "Type B" personality where they are more relaxed and easy going. Furthermore, some people have a little bit of both and be very detail oriented but also easy going. Even though there is no right or wrong leadership style, transactional leadership tends to be more common in the workplace. These type of individuals tend to care more about the end result of task completion rather than the journey of completing the task. One of the dangers in this leadership style is that the leaders become so focused on tasks that they are viewed as workaholics. Furthermore, they may even expect their employees to risk their personal lives to complete tasks. It is not dreadful to be focused and goal-oriented like most transactional leaders are. However, sacrificing one's personal life to achieve a work task is unbalanced. Pastor Hokes said that people whom are driven often pay a sacrifice. He said that there are many times when church leaders are so driven to accomplish tasks for their ministry that they sacrifice their personal relationships with their families. In fact, he said that he has seen many pastors treat their ministry as mistresses and give more to the ministry than they do their own wives and children. Any time we lead an unbalanced life, we are susceptible to allowing Satan to enter in and harm us. Once more, having an unbalanced life where we are putting more emphasis on work than personal life or vice versa is a symptom of unhealthiness. Many times our family lives are unhealthy and this draws us to putting an unhealthy amount of time into our work or our spiritual lives are unhealthy and we replace it with our work load. People whom live and unbalanced and unhealthy life have a difficult time functioning in the world. They tend to have physical, emotional, and psychological problems. God gives us specific instruction to live a balanced and healthy life. God even strived for balance when He created the world. In Genesis 2-2-3, the Bible states that God finished His work on the seventh day and rested. This shows that God wants us to have a balance in whatever we do, yet many people continue to struggle with balancing their lives. Transactional leaders must seek the understanding of what is contributing them to live unbalanced lives and correct this by focusing more attention on things that give them genuine pleasure. There are also dangers in the transformational leadership style. People whom have this leadership style tend to be laid back in their personalities which can often be mistaken as uncaring. Once more, employees may take advantage of their leader's patient and easy going nature and assume that the leader will overlook any major mistakes that they have made. Transformational leaders have to balance between being patient with their employees while setting strict guidelines for them to follow. If transformational leaders do not employ guidelines for their employees, then they will lose their respect. If leaders fail to set rules for and train their employees properly, they are doing their employees a disservice. Reflect on the example of King David in the Bible and his failure to rebuke his wicked sons. David did not give his sons the stable foundation to behave appropriately and he continuously overlooked their wrongdoings. As a result of David's parental negligence, his son Adonijah was executed by King Solomon after David died. Much like David, leaders whom take a nonchalant approach to leading are setting up their employees for failure. The interesting thing about both leadership styles is that if mishandled, there can be an imbalance in managing a team of employees. Pastor Hokes stated that it is always good to have balance when leading others. He said that there is nothing wrong with being driven and focused, but we also have to be patient with those whom we lead. Once more, he said that it is necessary to be patient with others but we must also be assertive and uphold our principles as leaders. Additionally, employees must be aware of which leadership style is most suited for them. Much like Rudy in the vignette, many people thrive under the leadership of a transformational leader. It is very important to know our own personality and work styles and consider how it fits with our supervisor. Pastor Hokes said that if he was counseling someone like Rudy, he would advise him to choose a leader that can get the best out of him. Unfortunately for many of us, we do not have the luxury of choosing our leaders and this can and has often led to conflict with them. In this case, it is very important for employees to assess their leaders' personality and work style even before they start the job. It is always a good idea to interview the supervisors as a prospective employee. It is not enough for the employer to ask all of the questions during the interview. We must also ask them questions to see if they will be a good fit for us. Even then we may acquire a supervisor whose leadership style does not work well with us. In this case, we should deeply consider how the leadership is impacting us and consider our options of expressing our concerns to our supervisor, transferring to another team, or resigning from the position. These things are not easy to do; however if we turn a blind eye to poor leadership or stay under leadership that will hinder our growth then we are at just as much fault as the leader.

*L'Orangerie Crawford & Terri Harrison*

## TRANSPARENT LEADER:

*Tammy is originally from New York but has accepted a job offer in London. It has been a bit of a culture shock for her, but she seems to be adjusting well. She has been working at this new job for 5 months now. One night she writes a letter to her sister Jessica which reads: "Hey Jess, how are you, Dan, and the kids? I hope all is well and tell them that I said hello and can't wait to see them for Christmas. Things are going well for me here. I've met some really nice people and even went out on a date last weekend. One thing that has been harder to adjust to is the weather. I thought upstate New York gets cold, LOL! Anyway, the new job is great! My coworkers are fabulous and are just about the nicest people you would ever want to meet. One coworker in particular, Rebecca, is just hilarious and I would love for you both to meet one another someday. My boss, Neil is amazing, OMG! He is so open to us coming to him for suggestions and he is always receptive of our input. He always provides us with the right amount of information that we need to complete a task rather than giving us just enough and then becoming annoyed when we need additional information or don't have the answers. Do you remember how horrible my boss was before I left New York? How he never wanted to help, always kept his door closed, and chewed us out if we went to other people for help? Well, Neil is the complete opposite. He takes the time to ensure that we are successful with our projects and he never, ever turns us away if we have genuine concerns. I couldn't be happier with him. Well, I'm just about finished talking about me. Love you much. Can't wait to see you and go shopping."*

*XOXO,*
*Tammy*

Transparent leadership is one of the most effective leadership strategies in business. Transparent leaders are defined as people whom offer help

*Healing in the Workplace*

to their employees why relinquishing power and asks for help from their employees. These type of leaders are fully engaged with all of their employees and always have their employees best interest in mind. One of the ways that transparent leaders motivate their employees is by building trust with them. When employees trust their leaders, they follow them wholeheartedly. Furthermore, transparent leaders have a passion for their employees and what they do. Transparent leaders have a zeal for their duties as leaders that inspire their employees to be enthusiastic about their jobs. Paul was such a leader. In the book of Acts, Paul's fire for Christianity inspired many to change their evildoings. Paul's leadership style teaches us that successful leaders always cares for the people that they are leading and cares for the message that they are transmitting.

It is God's will for leaders to get to a place where they can share their power with their subordinates. He created us to be relational; meaning that we can never do anything alone and by ourselves. This is particularly true for accomplishing tasks. When we have a goal or a task to achieve, we cannot do it alone. In fact, God did not design for us to complete our goals by ourselves. One of the authors remembered a time when she was told by a friend that his family was not helping him achieve a task. At first, the author agreed with his family that he should achieve his goal on his own because after all, he is an adult. In addition, his family told him that they achieved their goals on their own and he should do the same. However, after the Holy Spirit ministered to her, she realized that her friend's family was out of line with God. The first thing that she realized is that her friend's family was being untruthful in telling him that they achieved their goals on their own. God ministered to her by telling her that there is no one on this earth who has not had a door opened for them to achieve a task. God clearly told her that even if we lack the support of people, He still opens doors for us and allows us to accomplish things on a regular basis. The next thing that the author realized after being ministered to by God about her friend's family is that people whom lack the compassion to help others achieve a goal are often insecure and controlling. Once more, God told her that these type of people do not like to see others succeed out of fear that it will cost them something. Moreover, God told her that people like her friend's family like to see others downtrodden because it makes them feel better about their despondent lives. Pastor Hokes conquered with the author's illumination about her friend's family by suggesting that managers whom do not share the power with their employees and whom purposefully withhold information and help from their employees are controlling. Even further, he said that these type of managers do not have a true passion for their employees. Pastor Hokes said that David was so passionate for his people that he was willing to give his life for them. Managers or leaders that truly care about their employers will always give them the necessary tools and information to help them get the job done. Another reason that many managers withhold information from their employees is because they have a sense of entitlement and view their employees as their possessions rather than their helpmates. Pastor Hokes said that he has seen this scenario far too often in the church where many pastors become Lord over their churches. He said that many of these type of pastors believe that their congregation belongs to them and forget that they belong to God. Transparent leaders understand that their subordinates are not their possessions and encourage them to pursue their purpose even if that means that they have to move on to another job to do so. One other illumination that one of the authors received about her friend's family is that people whom really care about others will never close their door on someone who needs help. God enlightened her that people who do not guide others when they see that they need help are detached and coldhearted. People whom care about others never close their door; especially when they can teach others something that they know will benefit them. Transparent leaders go out of their way to teach their employees skills that they may not have because they feel a point of connection to them. When leaders have a closed door policy and do not want to share their knowledge with their employees, they are disconnected from others, from themselves, and from God. Pastor

*Healing in the Workplace*

Hokes said that he can recognize the connection that other pastors have with their congregation. He said that the pastors whom take the time to meet and greet their church members, or go out of their way to counsel them are the ones whom feel connected to them and do not want to be too far away from them. However, he said that pastors whom shy away from their churchgoers are disengaged and need a renewal of their mind and spirit. Once more, he said that ministry is always about reaching the people. Since many leaders are not transparent and have a difficult time connecting to their employees, organizations have to be careful about who they appoint into leadership positions. Not everyone is destined to be a leader and even when someone is ordained into leadership, it should not be taken for granted. Pastor Hokes said that leaders should never do anything without God's anointing. The Bible accounts for several leaders whom were successful and inspired their personnel. The one thing that they all have in common is that they had God's covering over their leadership. Transparent leaders; especially those whom are Christians should never forsake God's grace because this is what keeps them connected to their employees. Besides, Pastor Hokes eloquently reminded us that what makes noble leaders is the faith that people have in them.

## Scenario - *FAIR AND JUST LEADERSHIP*:

*At Roosevelt Middle School, a fight broke out between two 8th grade boys during lunch time. Mrs. Rosales, the 6th grade school counselor broke up the fight but did not witness who initiated it. Mrs. Rosales asked some of the children who were eating nearby if they had seen anything and they all said "no". Mrs. Rosales then took the boys to the Dean's office so that she could further investigate the situation......*

*Dean Brown: "Have a seat boys. I would like to talk to you for a minute. I had you both write a statement about what occurred during lunch and I would like to read it to you. Alex, you wrote that Mark*

99

was making fun of your younger sister and you told him to stop and he wouldn't. You also wrote that Mark told you that you had to make him stop and before you knew it, he ran over to you and began hitting you."

*(Mark interrupts and begins to dispute. Alex says that he is telling the truth. Dean Brown quiets the boys down by telling them that they each would have a turn to speak and commanded them to respect one another while in her office. She continues by reading Mark's statement which suggests that Alex initiated the fight).....*

Dean Brown: "There were no witnesses regarding who initiated the fight; however, Mrs. Rosales said that she saw you both hitting one another."

Alex: "But he was talking about my sister and I have to defend my family!"

Mark: "I wasn't talking about her and you jumped down my throat for no reason."

Dean Brown:"Okay boys. Now you know the school's policy on fighting. We don't tolerate fighting regardless of who started it. You boys know this already. If I believe you Alex that Mark started the fight without listening to Mark's side, then I wouldn't be fair and vice versa. I don't know who started the fight, but what I do know is that you both were fighting. This is not tolerated and you both are suspended for three days."

*(Mark and Alex groan and are visibly upset)*

Dean Brown: "Now, do you both understand why you are suspended? Please tell me."

Mark: "Because we were both fighting."

*Dean Brown:" Do you agree with this Alex?"*

*Alex:" Yes."*

*Dean Brown: "Okay, very good. Now, Mark please wait in the front office and Alex please go to Mr. Cooper's office while I call both of your parents."*

Fairness is one of the biggest issues that employees have with their managers. Employers have to be very careful that they are adhering to fair practices or they can be vulnerable to grievances. When employers violate fair practices, it can cause severe psychological damage and employees are left feeling betrayed. Leaders must question whether or not they are practicing fairness in the workplace. With the pursuit of reaching quotas or completing job duties, the issue of fairness can often go unnoticed. Employees' main concern regarding fairness is usually compensation and promotions. Employers should not overlook fairness because if they do, there can be negative implications. If employees perceive that they are being treated unfairly, they can become unhappy and this can result in high turnover and even an uprising against the organization. God wants leaders to be fair in their practices just like He is fair with us.

To be a successful leader, one has to be fair. Whether the setting is a small organization or a large fortune 500 company; effective management always keep the issue of fairness in mind. When leaders are unfair, they are often behaving selfishly and not thinking about the greater good of their team or department. One of the affects of unfair leadership is that it creates a negative organizational culture. Unfair practices among leaders set a precedence for how employees should treat one another. Pastor Hokes said that he has witnessed this in the church where a pastor would treat his wife or his staff unfairly and the church members would witness this. He said that shortly thereafter, the church members would start treating one another in the same manner. When leaders are unfair, they are not after God's own heart. When God appoints someone as a leader, He wants them to lead just as He does. In Jeremiah 3:15, the Bible states that God will give His people shepherds after His own heart and they will feed us with knowledge and understanding. Fair and just leaders understand that they have to earn the respect of their subordinates and not always earn their love. In the example of the vignette, Dean Brown did not seek out affirmation or love from the two young boys who she was counseling. Instead, she gave them both consequences for their misbehavior even though it was unpopular with the boys. As a result, the boys were not happy about her decision, but they knew that she was fair and respected her. Pastor Hokes revealed that respect for leaders goes further than love for them. He recalled times when his parents gave him and his siblings consequences for their behavior. He said that his parents were fair but not always popular with him and his siblings. Pastor Hokes said that his parents would always tell them that they will dislike them now but love them later. He explained that they meant that they, as the leaders of the family had to make unpopular decisions that the children would dislike now but love them for later because they were saving them from the hardships that come along with being disobedient. Often times, fair leaders have to make tough decisions that will benefit the team and not just one individual. As a result, they have to be willing to hold firm to their decisions even if they are disliked. Noah is one example in the Bible of having to stand alone because he did the right thing according to God. Noah was literally removed from the rest of the population because he decided to serve God and not live an unholy life. One of the reasons why leaders fall prey to unfairness and unholiness is because they are too weak to stand by themselves when others are doing wrong. Many leaders may see that their colleagues are mistreating their employees and to avoid any backlash from them, they behave the same way out of fear of sticking out like a sore thumb. Once more, many leaders want to be liked so badly by some of their employees that they favor them over other employees. It would have been easy for Dean Brown to

*Healing in the Workplace*

either choose one of the boy's side over the other or choose to not give them consequences at all. However, she was willing to do what was fair even if that meant that the boys and the boys' parents disliked her for it. In addition, people have to realize that when they fail as a leader, it is often because they have turned their back on God's instruction to them as leaders. God gives leaders a framework to follow when dealing with others. Pastor Hokes suggested that this framework starts off with living a holy life and putting God first, then caring for others, and then thinking of self as last. When leaders manipulate this framework and think of their needs first or are unfair with their employees, they are hurting their blessings. God wants all of His appointed leaders to prosper, but they are condemning themselves when they are mistreating their subordinates. He wants us to know that if He treats us fairly and He is the author of the universe, then we are not exempt from treating those whom are under our leadership with respect and equality.

## THINGS TO PONDER ON:

- There are many leadership styles that are exhibited within a company. Leaders are born and meant to nurture and cultivate. What type of leader are you? What type of leader do you want to become? Do you believe you are an effective leader? These questions are relatively simple but they are powerful nonetheless. When answered truthfully, the real journey begins. Are you willing to accept the challenge to be the born leader God has called you to be? ..........Genesis 49:10 and Numbers 33:1

- Leadership qualities are imparted from God to man. Leadership skills must meld together with the purpose of guiding a group to success. Being approachable, sensitive to others, as well as understanding are all important leadership qualities. Leaders are born but being a good and fair leader is a choice.......... Numbers 1:16

- A transparent leader is not afraid of letting others see his or her vulnerability. What you see is what you get with a transparent leader. When God chose leaders in the Bible, He always had a purpose and plan in mind. God's chosen leaders were expected to be open and honest with their constituents and have a heart and ear to listen to God for instruction. Are you a leader who seeks Godly instruction and can hear God? Search throughout the scripture and see if you are a transparent leader like Moses was in the book of Numbers........Numbers 7:1

- Transparency requires full relinquishing of self and a willingness to be led by the spirit of God. Although it is not an easy task, it is extremely necessary. God chose and gave Moses instruction but Moses was willing to hear from God. God molded Moses to be a transparent leader.......Numbers 7:2-3; 10

- Fair and just leadership is something that everyone expects to receive at the workplace. Unfortunately for many of us, this is not the norm. Not every leader knows how to treat employees fairly. Treating others with respect is the beginning of a fair and just working relationship........Romans 2:9-11

- Being impartial to staff is crucial in a fair and just leader. Impartiality is conducive to a healthy work environment and leads to successful benchmarks. Mutual respect goes a long way with staff. When staff recognizes the efforts made by leadership to implement an impartial, fair, just, and equitable work environment, a holistic workplace emerges. Jesus was a leader who was impartial and equitable in His treatment of others...........Ephesians 6:8-9

# ORGANIZATIONAL CLIMATE

Employees are constantly being influenced in organizations. Ideas, beliefs, and attitudes of the people in the organization are continuously challenged and affected. All of the influencing behaviors make up the organizational culture of a business. Although the culture of a company has been researched extensively, many people do not understand the meaning of organizational climate. Organizational climate, much like organizational culture refer to the environment in the work setting. However, the climate of an organization is arguably easier to change because it has yet to reach the collective, deeply held beliefs of the people in the organization. Organizational climate refers to the way people in the organization perceive how things should operate, while organizational culture is when people have developed a shared way of behaving that is rarely unchangeable. When thinking about organizational culture, consider the various cultures in the world. Each culture has its distinct way doing things and marked behavioral patterns that are passed down generationally. This can be said of organizational culture. Many organizations have adopted deeply rooted behavioral patterns and beliefs that are passed down from upper management to lower level employees. Organizational climate, on the other hand may not affect the entire organization, but just a department and/or a small group of people within the organization. The challenge that most consultants have when working to change a negative organizational culture or climate is that they have to toil with the schemas of the people within the organization. Schemas are the perceptions that one has about the world and themselves in the world. In other words, schemas are the outlook that one has on his or her environment. Business consultants are challenged with this because people's outlooks on their environment; particularly their work environment differ from person to person. Some people may have a positive outlook on their work environment as evidenced by them going out of their way to help colleagues complete their tasks while others may have a more negative outlook as evidenced by isolating themselves from others and/or speaking harshly to others at work. Whether one has a positive or negative outlook on the work environment, both perspectives can be infectious and can lead to the forming of organizational climate. The climate created in Sodom and Gomorrah is a prime example of how the negative outlooks of the people can impact the entire culture. The people of the city had negative distortions of sexual relationships as evidenced by the prevalence of homosexuality and sex crimes being committed. The sin was so great that it covered the entire land and God was forced to bring judgment against them and destroy the city. Much like Sodom and Gomorrah, a negative organizational climate can impact the entire business and destroy it. This is why it is important for organizations to work with change managers and/or business consultants to assess the healthiness of the organization and provide them with feedback and tools on how to improve the climate of the organization. If organizations fail to recognize when they need help, it can lead to its demise.

## Scenario - HAZARDOUS WORK ENVIRONMENT:

*EAC is a workforce placement agency that places unemployed individuals on temporary or permanent assignments. The building that houses the call center employees is very old and needs renovation. The electrical systems is outdated and there are numerous power outage; especially on windy days. During power outages, employees are asked to go home because all of the computers and telephone systems are shutdown. The plumbing has been an enduring problem as well. The sewage is so blocked up that it has developed a toxic smell throughout the office. Not to mention, there are rodents and cockroaches crawling in the break room, bathrooms, and on some of the employees' desks. The heating and air system is also outdated. When the air does work it is so cold that many of the employees develop muscle and joint pain and have even gotten sick and had to miss several days of work. Needless to say, the work conditions at this organization have slowed down productivity tremendously. Employees have even began to have a non- caring attitude about doing their job. They often complain to management but they respond to them by saying that they are "working on it". Some of the employees have even called OSHA to investigate the problem but the response has not been fast enough. Due to the horrendous work conditions, some of the employees are thinking about going to their union to file a complaint and/or a lawsuit.*

Occupational hazards can gravely affect organizations. Such hazards can come in the form of physical, chemical, biological, or emotional that has negative effects on employees. Safety and health hazards saturate the work environment and can harmfully impact the climate of the organization. Of course we know that there are legal implications for hazardous work environments; however there are ethical implications as well. Ethical organizations always keep the employees' safety and health in mind and they never turn a blind eye to unhealthy an unsafe work conditions. All employees have the right to work in safe environments and employers are obligated to provide safety and health measures, yet many organizations fail to do so. Organizations that do not care about the safety and health of the employees have created an unethical and immoral climate that goes against the principles of God. Before sustainability and global warming was popularized, God discussed issues of sustainability, ill-advised against abusing the land's natural resources, and required the people to protect the endangered. In the Old

Testament of the Bible, God gave specific instruction to the people to take pride and upkeep in the environment in not only which they lived but also in which they worked. The scriptures in Leviticus 25 gives us insight into God's love for the land and gives specific instruction to Moses on how to train the people to take care of the land in which they lived and worked. God teaches us that we must care about the safety and health of others; especially at work. In fact, God is even concerned with the life of a bird as shown in Deuteronomy 22:6-7. If God is concerned about the safety of a bird, there is no excuse for organizations to not care about the safety of employees. When employers do not care about the employees most basic needs, they are breaking the psychological contract that they have with them. The psychological contract refers to the unspoken, mutual expectations between the employers and employees. Employers expect that employees come to work on time and do their best to complete their duties, while employees expect to go to work, be safe, and receive compensation for their labor. The breaking of the psychological contract by the employers can result in the dissatisfaction of the employees. When employers break this contract by not providing a safe and healthy work environment, employees can become rightfully distressed. Even though working for organizations that do not care about its' employees safety can cause anyone to revolt, God instructs us that we have to still do things decently and orderly. People whom work in unsafe and hazardous environments, there are surely things that can be done that would not further jeopardize them. Pastor Hokes said that if he was counseling someone who works in unsafe conditions, he would advise him or her to get a petition going among the employees and involve the union, if applicable. He also said that most times, employees have difficulties in changing the environment because they do not put their concerns in writing. First Lady Hokes suggested that expressing concerns anonymously could be a great way to start changing this type of negative organizational climate. In addition, if the conditions persist even after being brought to the attention of upper management, unions, and governmental agencies, employees must then weigh their costs. In other words, employees must determine whether or not the conditions

*Healing in the Workplace*

are minor enough that they can endure the conditions until they find another job or if they are severe enough that they take legal action against their employer. If the hazards are minor, employees have to learn how to manage such conditions. For example, one of the authors recalled a time when the bathroom at one of the businesses for which she worked never had any soap in the dispenser. She said that she expressed this concern to the receptionist and to her supervisor and both told her that it would be fixed. Days and weeks went by and the complaint was never considered. The author said that instead of her taking this matter to upper management, she decided to bring a small bottle of soap from home and took it with her every time she went to the bathroom. She remembered that it was inconvenient for a moment, but the condition was not so terrible that she needed to cause an upheaval at work. Pastor Hokes supported this by saying that we sometimes have to stand still and learn how to manage and endure the unpleasant conditions that we are in. He also said that God does not expect us to lie over and take anything from anyone, but He does want us to endure. However, this example does not suggest that extreme hazardous work conditions should be overlooked. If the conditions are seriously affecting one's health and nothing is being done about it, then legal action against the organization is permissible. If someone is working in such conditions and believes that a lawsuit should ensue, the appropriate documentation is needed to support the lawsuit. Employees in extreme hazardous conditions must provide documentation that they have complained to their supervisors, upper management, human resources, unions, and outside governmental agencies. Once this documentation is provided, a legal representative can further assist them with the situation. The authors by no means are attempting to provide legal advice nor are they promoting lawsuits against one's organizations. However, the authors' efforts in this scenario is to show that if organizations take serious safety and health hazards too lightly, employees may have the right to take legal action against them. Once more, the authors recognize that minor work hazards like lack of soap in the bathroom does not warrant mayhem and can be endured by employees.

109

*L'Orangerie Crawford & Terri Harrison*

## SCENARIO - WORKPLACE VIOLENCE:

Mount Moriah A & M is a small, private University. The human resources department has devised a university wide survey on workplace violence to be given to all its employees. Some of the employees are certain that they can detect the signs and behaviors of work place violence while others are not so sure. Human resources will be using this survey as part of data collection to create and implement a workplace violence prevention program. Below is the survey:

1. How long have you been employed at the organization?
2. What is your position at the organization?
3. Have you ever had conflict with others at the organization? Yes/No
4. Do you think that workplace conflict is normal? Yes/No/I don't know
5. Have you ever witnessed aggressive behavior among your colleagues? (i.e. yelling, screaming, hitting, bullying, incivility) Yes/No
6. If you witnessed aggressive behavior among your colleagues as the third party, do you believe that this was harassment? Yes/No/I don't know
7. Do you think that verbal, emotional, or mental abuse is considered workplace violence? Yes/No/I don't know
8. Do you think that excessive touching or hugging is considered workplace? Yes/No/I don't know
9. Would you be afraid to speak to an administrator if you witnessed workplace violence? Yes/No/I don't know
10. Do you believe that workplace violence affects productivity? Yes/No/I don't know

In the wake of disgruntled employees shooting their colleagues, it is a wonder that any one of us feels safe enough to go to work.

*Healing in the Workplace*

Though this is not the norm, organizations must recognize the signs or and take precautionary measures against workplace violence. Most people; especially managers are certain that they know the signs of workplace violence; however many of them actually do not. Since most organizations still lack the proper guidance on the signs of workplace violence, employees are susceptible to adverse outcomes. Once more, violent acts in the workplace can have long lasting effects on the organization including an increase in stress-related disability, decrease in productivity, and increase in turnover. Although there are many examples of violence given in the Bible, God actually hates violence; especially against the innocent. In fact, Proverbs 6:16-17 states that God hates six things including a proud look, a lying tongue, hands that shed innocent blood, a heart that devises wicked plans and feet that are swift in running to evil, and one who sows discord among brethren. All of these six things essentially refer to violence that can occur in the workplace. Moreover, these six things will be further examined in the chapter.

Surveys are effective in helping employees better understand their knowledge about workplace violence. Furthermore, First Lady Hokes said that this is an excellent approach to open up dialogue about and help create solutions for violence in the work setting. When thinking of violence; particularly in the work environment, most people assume that it refers to physical attacks. However; most people do not understand that workplace violence goes beyond physical attacks and can actually occur beyond work borders. Reflecting back to Proverbs 6:16-17 and the six things that God hates; these things are all examples of workplace violence that people fail to acknowledge as being violent. First and foremost, violence is any aggressive, hostile, cruel, or powerful act taken against someone or something. If we were to all examine ourselves, we can find examples of when we behaved aggressively, hostile, cruel, or powerful against someone else, yet we may not call ourselves violent. The reality is that if we have engaged in such acts at any point in our lives, we were behaving violently. God despises this and convicts the hearts of Christians whom engage in these type of acts. One of the things that God hates is a proud look. This refers to someone who is arrogant and is a lover of self. Most people may question how this is a big deal and how this may even be seen as violent. The issue with a proud look or arrogant person is that they tend to belittle others to make themselves feel better. When done in the workplace, this is actually a violent act that most people do not recognize as being a sign of workplace violence. Another thing that God says that he loathes is a lying tongue. We all have lied at least once in our lives, but many of us have become habitual liars. In this case, lying has become so automatic that it is second nature. When people lie to or against one another by spreading rumors, this is actually a violent act in the workplace. Hands that shed the blood of the innocent is another thing that God hates, yet it is being done more and more frequently in the workplace. This does not just refer to the hurting and killing of innocent people at work, but it also suggests the psychological and emotional damage to colleagues. This can occur when one employee is berating another by using foul language or name calling. The fourth thing that God hates is a heart that devises wicked plans. People who devise wicked plans are always plotting and scheming to hurt others and/or get over on others. This can occur in the workplace when employees sabotage other people's work or backbite against one another. Most people would not accept this as being violence, but in fact it is a violent act in the workplace. Feet that are swift in running to evil is an extension of the previous act and is something that God detests. Examples of this in the workplace are people whom vandalize or steal their colleagues' property, or physically attack their colleagues by pushing, hitting, or raping them. Lastly, God despises others whom sow discord against brethren. Most people think of gossip when reflecting on this example of what God hates; however it can also refer to causing conflict among colleagues. There are many people that like to see others argue and dislike one another. In fact, these type of people will go out of their way to engage in "he-say, she-say" activity to stir quarrels among their colleagues. This is a violent act in the workplace because it can negatively affect others. It is important

*Healing in the Workplace*

to know the warning signs of such behavior and take action to protect oneself. Pastor Hokes said that he cautions people to look for violent signs in others and report it to someone in a position of authority. He also said that employees should look for disturbing pictures or words that their colleagues post on their walls. This could be a sign that the person is tormented and can behave violently at a moment's notice. People should also take threats seriously and document and report it. Once more, organizations can help decrease workplace violence by implementing safety committees that will create prevention and intervention policies. In addition, organizations need to train the staff on recognizing some of the basic signs and symptoms of the employees that are in distress or have mental health conditions. Some of these warning signs include frequent crying outbursts or anger outbursts, excessive absenteeism or lateness, distractibility, poor hygiene, isolation from others, and overreaction to things. People must acknowledge that mental health issues are real and if untreated, not only does the person with mental health problems suffer but others around them suffer as well. In fact, in 1 Timothy 4:1, the apostle Paul preaches that many will give into deceiving spirits and doctrines of demons. People whom suffer from mental health problems need cleansing of their spirit and the counsel of professionals that can help them work through their difficulties. In addition to organizations having a responsibility of decreasing workplace violence, employees are also obligated. One of the things that employees can do to decrease workplace violence is recognize that any aggressive, hostile, cruel, or condescending action is violent. Whether a person is aggressive or passive-aggressive, both behaviors can lead to violence and should be eliminated in the workplace. Once more, employees need to understand that workplace violence can occur outside of work. One of the authors recalled a time someone told her that he was having conflict with a fellow colleague. He told her that one day, he went to a function outside of work and shared his thoughts and feelings about this colleague to another colleague who happened to be at the same function. He said that unbeknownst to him, this colleague was so offended by what he said about the other colleague that she reported him and he was placed on administrative leave for harassment. People must understand that these type of situations are considered to be third-party harassment and have serious and devastating repercussions. Pastor Hokes said that when possible, it is best to leave issues about the job at the job. However, he acknowledged that people often form personal relationships with others at work in which they share their most intimate thoughts and feelings. Pastor Hokes suggested that we should only share such personal feelings about the job with others whom we have a personal relationship and not other colleagues that we do not know well because they can become offended and take action against us. There are several things that can be done about workplace violence. We all have a duty to recognize the signs within ourselves and others and get the necessary help. Work alone can be stressful, but no one deserves to be stressed over the possibility of violence erupting at the workplace.

## Scenario - PERSONALITY DIFFERENCES:

*Barbara, is generally a happy and easy going person. She often wakes up with a positive attitude on life. She is known around the office for her energetic presence and beautiful smile. If her colleagues were to describe her personality, they would say that she is an extrovert and she always knows how to make someone's day a little brighter. Nash is the complete opposite of Barbara. He is pessimistic and tends to wake up with a negative disposition. He keeps to himself at work and when confronted by his colleagues about a report or assignment, he usually responds harshly. If his colleagues were to describe him, they would say that he has a prickly personality and is not very well liked. Barbara and Nash both have positions in which others have to interact with them to complete tasks. Employees do not mind going to Barbara because they know that she is likely to help them if she is able. Nash, however is a different story. The employees do not like going to him because his moods are so unpredictable. One minute he is angry and then the other he is highly anxious. In addition, when Nash participates on projects, he is*

*Healing in the Workplace*

*very argumentative and uncooperative, causing the task to be delayed. Some of the employees have even resorted to circumventing Nash and requesting assistance from others. Many of the employees wonder why Nash has not been fired yet but the truth is that he is smart and good at what he does.*

Personality differences are an important part of diversity in the workplace. If everyone behaved the same and looked at things in the same way, things would be pretty boring around the office. Working with someone who has perspective on life that differs from yours can be exciting because this person can offer his or her unique experiences to enrich your life. There are five major personality styles that have emerged in the field of psychology. Extravert is one of the personality styles that refer to someone who is outgoing and assertive. Another personality style that describes someone who is kind and has good problem solving skills is called Agreeableness. Openness is a personality trait that is much like Agreeableness; however this type of person is flexible and genuinely open to other people's ideas. The Conscientious personality trait refers to someone who is highly organized and detail oriented while the Neurotic personality is someone who is highly anxious and insecure. Though these different personality traits make the work environment unique, it can also make the work environment difficult if people are unaware of how to manage one another's personality traits. Once more, if people do not learn to work and communicate with people whom have different personalities than their own, it can cause conflict and negatively affect the organizational climate. Jesus' disciples is a wonderful example of different personality traits coming and working together. The apostle Paul was very zealous and determined while the apostle Thomas was more logical and reserved. Surely, these two personality differences made for some disagreements, but they did not allow their different perspectives deter them from their mission and did not allow their differences to infect the climate of their work environment.

Most people confuse behaviors with personality. Certainly, personality traits can be a driving force to one's behavior, but it is only a small part of the equation. There are several factors that go into someone's behavior such as the need to survive. For example, a person can be a generous and honest person in almost all instances, but let's say that he lost his job and did not have enough money to feed his children. Now imagine that this person legitimately found some money lying around. Instead of turning it in to authorities, he might keep the money to buy food for his family. Now the question is if this person's personality has changed to being dishonest now that he committed this act to feed his family. Most people would argue that if he was truly an honest person then he would have turned in the money regardless of his circumstances; however others may say that this does not change his personality because he did what he did to meet a basic need. Once more, people can have a combination of personality traits that make it difficult to characterize them solely on their behavior. This is important because employers need to know how to manage behaviors and not personalities. However, most managers fail because they attempt to change their employees' personality rather than extinguishing misbehaviors. When managers attempt to change personalities rather than behavior, it can affect the work environment because employees will begin to feel devalued. It is important for organizations to implement training on coping with personality differences so that people can learn to understand their differences rather than attempt to change them. Even the most difficult personality, though not easy, can be dealt with in the workplace. For example, dealing with someone like Nash in the scenario is complex because this type of personality is more on the Neurotic side. Knowing that a person who is Neurotic is more likely to be anxious, pessimistic, and insecure, it is highly important to communicate with this type of person in such a way exhibits tolerance and patience. This does not mean that we must walk on egg shells around this type of personality; however we must understand that this type of person is already internally fragile. Furthermore, we have to understand that when someone with this personality trait lashes out and criticizes us, though it may feel hurtful,

*Healing in the Workplace*

the criticism that they give to themselves is far worse. First lady Hokes said that we have to understand to adjust and learn to deal with people's character flaws. She said that we have to show these type of people compassion and understand that they are likely to have dealt with major challenges in their lives that contributed to their difficult personalities. This does not mean that we have to act as someone's therapist and analyze their lives; however we should have some discernment into what they might be going through. First Lady Hokes said that as Christians, we have to be in tune with God so that we can be in tune with His people. Meaning, we cannot be so into our flesh that we fail to discern when someone is going through a difficult time and may need a word of encouragement or even a hug. Even further, people do not have to have a Neurotic personality to be struggling with things in their personal lives that they take out on others around them. We must always offer our support in such cases even if that person may have lashed out at us at an earlier time. Again, we have to understand that this person is likely fragile inside and may be searching for comfort. This is not to say that it is easy to comfort a colleague who is having challenges or who has a Neurotic personality. In fact, we may even feel the urge to give that person a piece of our minds. Some people may even struggle to show compassion to someone who has lashed out at them and although this is a natural, human response, it is ungodly. God expects us to still practice compassion toward one another. Pastor Hokes said that in such cases, we should not take someone's lashing out as a personal attack even though it may feel personal. We have to remember that we all have different coping styles to deal with larger problems. Some of us retreat inward and isolate while others lash out. We must learn to communicate effectively when someone is in this state of mind. It is foolish to argue with this person and tell him or her that they are wrong no matter how tempting because this person is unreasonable at the moment. Instead, it is better to conduct ourselves as the Bible instructs us in Proverbs 15:1 and give a soft word to turn away wrath. Surely, this takes practice and we may even stumble and engage in an argument with someone who is being difficult; however we must continue to try to show them love.

*L'Orangerie Crawford & Terri Harrison*

Although Nash's personality type is more likely to cause problems in the workplace, someone with Barbara's personality can also be challenged. Barbara's personality can be categorized as Agreeableness. She and others like her may be a joy to work around; however there may be some people that do not like her personality. First Lady Hokes said that there are some people that may say that people like Barbara are too nice and may even find working with them to be unpleasant. In such cases, it is important that people like this understand that not everyone will appreciate their kindness nor will they be kind to others in the same way. Though this is disheartening, it is a reality. Not everyone, even Christians, will live holy lives in accordance with God's word. We must understand that people, even when saved and filled with the Holy Spirit will allow themselves to struggle with the vices that kept them in bondage when they were unsaved. Unfortunately, some people will not allow themselves to let go of the vicious thinking. In such cases, people like Barbara must pray for those whom do not appreciate kindness and may even take advantage of kindness. The reality is that people that do not appreciate someone's kindness has an unholy heart and needs a renewing of the mind. Moreover, Pastor Hokes said that we cannot allow someone else's unholiness and negative outlook on life infect us and make us become bitter. If we feed into someone else's poor behavior or thinking then we are not doing our jobs as Christians. Pastor Hokes said that our job as Christians is not to focus on winning the battle but winning the war which is to live holy and kind toward others to win souls for God's kingdom.

## THINGS TO PONDER ON:

- The workplace is the last place one would think of being hazardous. In the book of Genesis, the environmental workplace matter is addressed. When God created the earth, He intended for man to care for it, to replenish not deplete the land. This

*Healing in the Workplace*

is the first introduction to environmental responsibility of man..........Genesis 2:15

- Everyone in the workplace is required by God to maintain a hazardous free environment. Once more, we all should care about one another's well-being at work. God gives clear instruction on how to maintain a hazardous environment to help eradicate sickness and disease..........Deuteronomy 23:14

- The earth was intended for man to work the land and enjoy the fruits of their labor. God never intended for violence to enter into the workplace. The workplace must be free from violence in order to thrive. The Lord gives us dominion over the earth but not over people..........Genesis 6:5, 11-12

- Workplace violence is ugly, it never prompts goodness, and it aims to destroy and victimize. What is your goal for the workplace? The Lord has plans for His children to prosper and reap a bountiful harvest from the efforts of the use of one's hands. Much too often, employees forget to do their job unto the Lord and completely remove the Lord from the equation of work. Employees must put the Lord first even while at work. Without a Godly focus workplace violence will come in like a flood. We must be willing to ask God to make us peacemakers.........Matthew 5:9

- Personality differences are prevalent in the workplace and cannot be eliminated. However, they can be managed. Managing personalities in the workplace requires effective leadership to lead and manage such differences discreetly, respectfully, and timely. The Lord understands differences in personality since He created all of us in a unique way.........Ephesians 5:1-33

- Personality conflict in the workplace is as serious as all other workplace issues. When conflict and strife of any kind is within the company, have the outlook of this being a great opportunity to lead by example. For instance, be the person who approaches the offended and ask for forgiveness wholeheartedly. Do not do this for popularity of others but because the Lord instructs this type of action. Being obedient is difficult at times but can you stand the risk of the sacrifice of not obeying? The consequence of disobedience might not be seen immediately but you can rest assured that the price will be far greater than setting pride aside and asking for forgiveness........Acts 2:38

# THE SOCIETAL
# OUTCAST

The workplace is much like high school. As disheartening as it sounds, we will never escape high school drama. If you think about it and look around your work office, you will see many of the same things that you have witnessed and/or have been subjected to in your high school years. Just like in high school, you may see many of the employees "hooking up" with one another and just like in high school, you may see the "popular" employees hanging out with one another, excluding the entry of anyone that does not fit their mold. Once more, just like in high school you may see people who do not fit in with everyone else and are considered to be outcasts. For these people, it may seem like a never ending cycle from teenage to adulthood. Many of them question which profession or job is right for them considering that they are "different" from others. What's even more discouraging is that people who are labeled as "outcasts" are made to feel strange and different by others. Some of the traits that people who are considered to be outcasts have is that they dress differently, behave differently, and even sound differently. This can be off-putting for others because we have been made to conform to many of society's traditions and customs. Think about the 1950s during the big industrial boom. Many Americans were moving to the suburbs and everyone's houses looked the same. Once more, everyone teenager aspired for the American dream to acquire 2.5 children with a house with a white picket fence around it. Not only

121

did people aspire to have the same things during this time, people also were expected to have the same beliefs and attitudes. In today's society, things have changed dramatically. Now, you can look around and see the uniqueness and individuality in all of us. The issue that many people have with this is that people's differences are still looked at as nonconformity. What many people do not realize is that God admires and even in some circumstances, requires us to be "different" from others. What He does not like; however is rebellion. God clearly tells us in Romans 12:2 that we should not be conformed to this world but be transformed by the renewing of our minds. This suggests that God wants us, especially Christians to not behave the same way the world does nor dress or even talk the same way that nonbelievers do. Instead, He wants us to have renewal of our minds and hearts so that we can show God's goodness and perfect will to the world. There were several types of people in the Bible whom were the "outcasts" in society. Many of them included prostitutes, tax collectors, and people ridden with sickness and disease. The interesting thing that we can find in the Bible is that Jesus even embraced these individuals and many of them were led to the kingdom. God wants us to be like Jesus and embrace the people that are considered to be outsiders on our job. Though we may think that we have nothing in common with them and they look and act differently than us, God still wants us to show them love. If we do not accept them, then we are being rebellious against Jesus' teachings. Even if we do not agree with their current or even their past lifestyle, we are not to judge them, but instead show them God's love through us.

## Scenario - CRIMINAL RECORD AFFECTING EMPLOYMENT:

*Keith is 26 years old with a wife and young child, Keith Jr. Keith is handsome, well built, smart, and personable. He made a mistake when he was 19 years old that got him in trouble with the law. One day, Keith and a friend were joy riding at 12 a.m., and his friend stopped at*

*Healing in the Workplace*

*a liquor store but told him to stay in the car. Keith did not know that his friend had a gun and was planning to rob the store. Keith heard gun shots and panicked. His friend came running out of the store with two bottles of liquor and some cash in his hand. Keith screamed at his friend saying, "what did you do?" "Did you kill someone in there?" "What have you gotten me into?" Keith and his friend sped off from the scene but shortly thereafter a police car pulled up behind them with the sirens roaring. Keith and his friend pulled over and were arrested. Witnesses from the scene had identified Keith and his friend as the robbers of the store. The police told them of this fact and Keith broke down and cried. Keith later took a plea deal that would have him serve six years even though he had no involvement in the crime. Keith did his time and was released from prison when he was 23 years old. Unfortunately, he had no skills but had a criminal record. Keith met his wife and they had Keith Jr. He knew that he now had to face the responsibility of supporting a family. Keith has been working odd jobs for several years now and has made just enough money to pay for grocery and minor bills. His wife is the primary bread winner and this leaves Keith feeling emasculated. He has tried to find full time work but no one would hire him because of his record. He wants to put his past behind him but it always seems to haunt him. Keith is fed up with his life and is contemplating joining an old friend and hustling in the street. One night, Keith was so overwhelmed that when he got home he barely spoke to his wife and child and went straight to his room. He lied on the bed and looked at the ceiling. He suddenly heard a voice calling his name. He first thought that it was his wife calling him but the voice appeared to be much deeper. He distinctly heard the voice say: "Keith, my son. All things are possible through me. You must have the faith of a mustard seed. I am your strength and you shall not want." Shaken by this, Keith dropped to the floor, belted out a loud cry and began praising the Lord. The next day, Keith told his wife what had happened and they both began crying.*

When one thinks about their employment opportunities, the usual concerns are: "Am I educated enough?" or "Am I skilled enough to perform the duties?" Though these are necessary questions to ask oneself when a job opportunity arises, there is one question that millions of people constantly have to ask themselves as it relates to entering the job market. Roughly 1 in 31 adults are paroled or on probation every year, according to a press release from the Pew Charitable Trust. These people are faced with putting the pieces to their lives back together which usually involves finding legitimate employment. The concern that many of these people have is whether or not employers will hire them because of their criminal past. This leaves many of them disconcerted. Once more, many of them may even have thoughts of going back to their old lifestyles because the prospect of obtaining a lawful job seems hopeless. However, God is a God of hope and just when we think that we are defeated, He steps right in to open pathways for us. Since God is such a forgiving God, we must come to a place where we can forgive ourselves, no matter how severe the transgression is that we have committed. First Lady Hokes said that people whom have a criminal record and are attempting to turn their lives around should never give up on themselves. Once more, she said that people around them like family and friends should keep them lifted up in prayer and encourage and support them as best as they can. Pastor Hokes followed up by saying that the most important part of these people's lives is what they have left and what they can do with what they have left. God says in His word that we all have a purpose. Even the crimes that one has committed has a purpose in God's perfect plan. It may be confusing to many people that God would allow someone's crime to be used for good, but He has given us plenty of examples that He can. In the book of Joshua, Rahab was a harlot or a prostitute that was used by Joshua to hide the men that he sent to spy on the city of Jericho. Because of Rahab's faithfulness, she and her family was spared and she was allowed to live amongst the Israelites. This example shows us that God is committed to us even if we have a shifty past. This; however may be a concept that many people have a difficult time dealing with; especially when they have been passed over numerous of times because of their crimes. The first thing that people in this situation must do is to look within themselves and address what caused them to commit the crime in the first place. This is not to say that they should ruminate on it to the point that they condemn themselves, but in order to truly change, they must understand what led them to making such a life altering decision in the first place. Often times, people commit crimes when they are young in age. The unfortunate thing about this is that most of the crimes are so devastating that it affects their lives in the long run. Pastor Hokes shed some light on this particular issue. He said that as a previous youth pastor, he has seen children and young adults make mistakes that affect them for the rest of their lives. He said that the reason being so is because most young people have poor judgment. Once more, most young people do not have the maturity to discern whether or not a situation could destroy their future or even their lives. This is why having a prayer life and devoted relationship with God is so important. When we stay prayerful and listen to God's voice, He tells us when we should not go to a certain place or be around a particular person because He knows that we can find ourselves in serious trouble if we do so. In addition to having poor judgment, many people in their older years commit crimes and are often repeat offenders. Many of these people cry out to the Lord for forgiveness and ask God that if He would spare them this one time, then they would change their ways. The alarming thing about this is that many of them find themselves right back in the same lifestyle committing crimes. Pastor Hokes said that in cases like this, many people have not truly hit rock bottom and have not become sickened by the negative lifestyle that they live. He said that in order for people to truly change, they have to be like the Prodigal son and become so downtrodden that the only thing that they could do is to turn to God for help. He also said that in order for us to be delivered from our demons, we must be disgusted with our old selves and look to God to renew us. More importantly, people in this circumstance must put themselves in a position to be strengthened daily, otherwise it would be tempting to go back to old, destructive habits. First Lady Hokes said that if you are discouraged because you cannot find a job because of your criminal past, you have to fill yourself up with God's word daily. She said that people in this situation have to go to weekly Bible study, prayer groups, and attend church frequently. She said that building up one's spirit will help them deny the temptations of the flesh and not want to go back to their old lifestyle. Moreover, it is crucial that the loved ones of these individuals support their efforts in living a Godly and straighten arrow life. If one truly loves their family or friend and knows that he or she is vulnerable because of their past lifestyle, they should never encourage them to engage in ungodly or criminal activities. If one does encourage them to misbehave then they are sending a clear message that they do not love nor care for them. It is so important for people whom are vulnerable because of their past issues to be around people whom will edify and want the best for them and not persuade them into doing the wrong things. In the case of Keith in the vignette and others in his position, it is critical that their significant others do all that they can to help build their self-esteem. This may mean that they will have to help them create their resume, take them on job interviews, or give them words of encouragement even if they have been repeatedly rejected by prospective employers. Pastor Hokes gave his testimony of a time when he was unemployed because of the unstable industry in which he was working in the early 1990s. He said that when he was working, the compensation and benefits were great, but he was constantly on shaky ground because the job was unpredictable. He said that when he was unemployed, he felt much like Keith did in the vignette. He said that he felt emasculated and unworthy and would even say that most men feel this way when they are not able to provide for their families. Pastor Hokes said that the one thing that helped him get through his feelings of depression was the support of his wife. He said that she never made him feel less than or guilty for not having a job. He also said that she gave him words of encouragement and continued to make him feel as if he was the head of the household. Pastor Hokes said that he wanted to share his personal testimony with other men whom are currently unemployed and feel emasculated because they currently cannot provide

*Healing in the Workplace*

for their families because he wants to give them hope. He said that even when things seemed hopeless at the time, God turned his situation around and can do the same for other men out there. Once more, he said that with the help of a loving woman, they too can get back on track. The one thing; however that men have to submit to is receiving help from their wives and not allow Satan to trick them into thinking that receiving help from a woman makes them weak. God created women to be men's helpmates and it is truly a beautiful thing when a man can admit that he needs help. Issues in relationships arise when some men have a difficult time receiving help from their wives and either isolate themselves or overcompensate by challenging them or over exerting their power because they feel unworthy. God wants men whom are unemployed and feel emasculated to know that it is more powerful to follow the wisdom of their wives instead of listening to others whom do not have their best interest at heart. Once more, it is a sin to challenge one's wife or even take your frustrations out on her by abusing her physically, mentally, or emotionally because you are feeling inadequate because of your lack of employment. Instead, understand that God is sending you on a journey to be transformed and that your wife is there to help you reach your purpose. For people whom are having challenges with finding employment because of their criminal past, there is hope. One of the things that is important to know is that most employers do not give background checks on prospective employees and even if they do, they usually are looking for crimes committed within the last 7 to 10 years. This means that a criminal record does not necessarily have to be disclosed unless the employer insists. If the employer does insist then the truth should be disclosed but an explanation of how the experience changed one's life for the better could be suffice. Once more, if crimes were committed as a child, juvenile records are sealed in some, if not in all states. If employment is denied because of a criminal record, one must understand that it may have been due to the type of job for which they were applying and the nature of the crime committed. For example, some sex crimes prohibit individuals from working with children. One must understand this and attempt to find a job or trade

*L'Orangerie Crawford & Terri Harrison*

in a field that does not involve children. In addition, one of the most important things that someone can do in this circumstance is gather resources to help them work through employment barriers. Most metropolitan cities have work source programs that help people with criminal records with building skills and obtaining job leads. Your local social services office should be contacted for further information. The one thing that God wants people in this position to know is that He will never forsake them. Even when things look bleak, He is still there, waiting to be called upon for help.

## Scenario - PERSONAL IMAGE AND WORKABILITY:

*Shelby County Employment Center has a strong reputation within its city. Hundreds of people go to the center every week in hopes of being placed out to companies for employment. Janine has been one of the center's clients for three weeks now. She was fired from her job as a waitress at a cafe downtown. Her employment recruiter asked her to complete several assessments to help distinguish which type of job would be best suited for her. The results of her assessments suggested that she had strong customer service skills. Her employment recruiter that he had the perfect job for her as a receptionist at a daycare center. He place Jeanine at the job and she began work shortly thereafter. Jeanine showed up to work on the first day and was introduced to the office manager, Carol. Carol was taken aback and put off by Jeanine's appearance. Jeanine is heavily tattooed on her arms and legs. She likes to think that they are a work of art. Carol was torn because she like Jeanine's personality but she knew that the children's parents at the daycare center would be opposed to Jeanine's appearance. The following morning Carol contacted Jeanine's employment recruiter and asked him to replace her.*

Personal image is a major concern and sometimes problem for employers. Many employees have to follow strict guidelines for how they present

*Healing in the Workplace*

themselves, depending upon the organization. When an employee does not follow such guidelines, there could be two things that they are communicating. The first thing is that they are rebellious and do not respect the authority of their employers. The other thing that they are communicating is that they likely have a negative self-image. Both of these attitudes toward following the image guidelines of the employer are irreverent. God commands us all to respect the decisions of authority and to have a positive self-image and self-worth. Having a poor image can seriously damage one's employment opportunities. Employers believe that if one does not care about his or her own image then they could not surely care about the organization and the clients. If one cannot adhere to the image guidelines of one's employer or if one cannot put together a positive, personal image for a job interview then one's success is highly unlikely.

In today's society, tattoos are inescapable. Many of us can attest to knowing someone with a tattoo or even having a tattoo ourselves. Regardless of one's own personal attitude about tattoos, they are not going away. Once more, with the media attention that many celebrities receive because of their tattoos, children are being encouraged to tattoo their own bodies. Even though many people with tattoos are employed and even have high ranked professional positions, tattoos can have a negative impact on employment opportunities. Employers are not allowed to discriminate against employees' style of dress if it is done for religious purposes. For example, Jewish and Muslim people are allowed to wear their traditional garb since it is an expression of their religion and culture. However, employers do have the right to impose rules against exposing tattoos if they are deemed to be detrimental for the company's image. Employees can choose to wear long sleeve shirts or long paints to cover their tattoos if their employers oppose to them exposing them. The issue is that some employees believe that they should not have to cover up their tattoos just to work on a job. What these individuals need to understand is that employers choose to hire them. They are not forced to hire them and at any given moment, they can be replaced. As harsh as

129

this may sound, it is the truth. Just like employees have the right to not work at a company, a company has the right to not allow an individual to work for them. This means that if employees value their position within their organization, then they must adhere to the organization's rules. Pastor Hokes said that Jeanine in the vignette and people with attitudes like Jeanine have to make a decision on what is more important to them: showing their tattoos or staying employed. Once more, he said that we all should stop putting our value on the wrong thing. This means that it is Jeanine's right to have tattoos, but it is not her right to force her employer to accept them. More importantly, people should find ways to strategically place their tattoos if they insist on having them. For example, discrete and hidden places on the body in which tattoos can be placed is not an issue for most employers. The issue comes when people get tattoos in areas such as the face that cannot be concealed. One of the authors recalled watching a television show in which this one young man was looking for employment in his town. He had several tattoos all over his body, including on his face. He explained to the reporter that it was a decision that he made when he was young, but now regrets because no one would hire him. He later told the reporter that he is looking into tattoo removal for his face so that he can get a decent job. This shows that one should never make a commitment to something that they can later regret in the future. In fact, many older people whom received tattoos when they were younger now regret the decision because they have experienced how it can hold them back from promotions and entering into new, coveted positions in their organizations. Pastor Hokes revealed the issue with tattoos from a Christian perspective. He said that committing to a tattoo is like entering into a covenant, much like a covenant between a man and his wife. He said that it is a covenant because quite often, blood is shed and every time God made a covenant with Israel, He signed it with blood. This is why many people later regret their tattoos and why the tattoo removal business is on the rise because people are entering into a covenant without thinking about the potential consequences. Whether one believes that tattoo is ungodly or not, all is not lost of one does have a tattoo. One can choose to not enter into some

*Healing in the Workplace*

industries in which a strict business dress code is required or one can choose to cover up the tattoos. What is most important in this case is that people understand that there are rules to be followed, some of them unspoken and some of them spoken. If one's employers outright tells says that visible tattoos are prohibited, then one can either follow the rule or move on. Meanwhile, if there is no strict rule against the exposure of tattoos, then employees still have a responsibility to take pride in their personal self image and present themselves with respect. First Lady Hokes said that when she was a Sunday school teacher working with youth, she would always tell the children that the way that they present themselves does in fact suggest how they feel about themselves. If people do not take pride in their appearance then they really do not have pride in themselves and the unfortunate part about this is that they may never be allowed to show their talent on a job just because they have problems with their personal presentation. God does not want us to be turned away from a position because we fail to present ourselves professionally. We must understand that although He was the one who gave us our talent, we have to put our best foot forward to show people our talent and not be distracted by a poor self image.

## Scenario - *THE NOT SO RETIREE:*

*Earl has given 30 years of service as a janitor for the Santa Fe School District. On this day, Earl could not be more thrilled. He is having his retirement party. He is looking forward to being at home with his wife and traveling the world with his grandchildren. About two months after his retirement, his wife was walking across the street to attend her weekly knitting class and was suddenly struck and killed by a drunk driver. Earl received word of this a few hours later and was devastated. He lost the love of his life and would be in an insurmountable amount of debt from the memorial. He is receiving a pension as a retired janitor but it is not enough to cover all of his expenses. He was now faced with the devastating thought of having to go back to work. He later found a job at serve mart, the local produce store. However, two and a half months later he was fired because his supervisor said he could not keep up with the demands of the job. One day, he called Employment Development Department and was crying uncontrollably over the phone. He told the representative that he was discourage, angry, and depressed. He even told the representative that he no longer had a reason to live. The EDD representative was so disturbed and concerned by Earl's report, that he began praying with him and gave him words of encouragement.*

Transitions are arguably the hardest thing to handle in life. Transition from high school to college, from college to employment, or from employment to retirement are all milestones, yet they are difficult to cope with. Change is a part of life that we must accept. Most people have a tough time accepting the changes that come in their lives because they are not looking at the positive aspects of the change. Change requires the letting go of what once was and the letting go of how things used to be. Though the difficulty of letting go of the past is human nature, God can help us work through the many changes that occur in our lives. Joshua experienced a transition in his life after Moses died. In Joshua 1:1-9, God spoke to Joshua appointing him to lead the children of Israel as Moses' successor. This was a major change in Joshua's life because he was no longer Moses' assistant but he was now the "big man in charge". God later told him to be strong, courageous, and not afraid because God was with him. Just like Joshua, God is with us when we transition into uncharted territory. He assures that he will not give us more than we can handle and that He has purposed the changes in our lives to make us stronger.

Some people dread the transition to retirement because to them it means that they are no longer useful and needed. This change can bring about things like anxiety, depression, and even boredom. Undoubtedly, it is a major change in one's life but it does not have to be a bad thing.

*Healing in the Workplace*

When many people reach retirement age, developmentally they begin to ponder on their lives and on whether or not they have made a difference and have accomplished the goals in which they sought out. When people of this age come to the conclusion that they have not achieved their purpose, they can be left feeling empty. Pastor Hokes said that many people of retirement age are looking for self worth. However, he said that we must understand that our lives are based on seasons and be comfortable in the season that God has put us in at the moment. One of the reasons why many people whom retire become cantankerous is because they have not embraced their season that they are in. One of the ways that people can embrace the "retirement season" is by learning to reinvent themselves and find meaning in what their life at the moment. In other words, many retired people can give back to younger people by imparting their wisdom and experience in a particular profession. The authors thought about an older man in their church who gives boxing lessons to youth in his neighborhood. Although he no longer has to work, he seeks enjoyment out of giving back to children and young adults. Another reason why some people whom are retired become angry or sad is because they are grieving the loss of their professions and whom they have known themselves to be. First Lady Hokes said that many people have the same experiences as Earl in the vignette did. She said that many people find themselves retired and shortly thereafter will lose a spouse or someone close to them. She said that in such cases, people are not only grieving the loss of a job but the loss of a loved one as well. People in this situation must recognize that their anger, depression, or anxiety is a sign of grief and that it is normal. Some Christians may believe that grieving is abnormal and may even be a sin; however this is false. Grieving is not a sin and is quite normal. In John 11:34-35, Jesus even grieved the death of Lazarus. There are many things that people can do to cope with their grief, even the grief of being retired. One of the things that people can do is join a support group and listen to the stories of others in similar situations. In fact, God frequently talks about the power of two or more coming together. Ecclesiastes 4:9-10 says validates the value of a friend and that two are better than one and if one fails, then the other will lift him up. This is exactly what support groups can offer individuals whom are grieving because of retirement. Some people may also have difficulty with retirement because of their outlook on life. They have lost an appreciation for the time that God has blessed them with. Pastor Hokes said that people have to remember that growing old is a privilege and is not promised. There is beauty in getting older and wiser and people have to rediscover who they are without the job. This is a time when people should reflect and explore whom they are outside of what they have done professionally. Pastor Hokes said that the true test that someone has discovered who they are in Christ is when he can talk about himself without mentioning his profession. People in retirement have to get back to rediscovering themselves much like a newborn baby discovers himself. Babies are constantly looking at their hands and their feet and wondering what their fingers and toes are for. They also look at surrounding objects and try to make meaning out of them. Retired individuals must have the same attitude and explore themselves and the beauty around them. This can happen by completing an unfinished goal or taking a trip that was put off for several decades. It can even happen by mending broken relationships with loved ones and asking for their forgiveness and giving them forgiveness. God wants us to live a peaceful and meaningful life in our latter days. If we have not always done right by our children or our spouses, we can make up for it by making amends and drawing nearer to them during this time. In Ecclesiastes 12:1, God tells us to remember Him in our youth so that we can have pleasure in our latter days. Some people are miserable in their latter years because they have lived an unholy life in their youth. However, God can turn this around if we come to Him and ask Him to help us live holy and righteous in our older years. Pastor Hokes said that he tells his congregation that it is more important to live a fulfilled life than a full life. Once more, it is more important to be proud of who you have become as a person than to be proud of the things that you have accomplished. What good is it to achieve goals if you have been an evildoer your whole life? One of the ways in which we can live a fulfilled life even in our retirement years is to set new goals for ourselves.

*Healing in the Workplace*

We can do this by creating a vision board and organizing our time to meet these goals. It may be a goal to go mountain climbing, or run in a marathon, or even teach our grandchildren how to drive. Whatever the goal may be, we should envision ourselves accomplishing the goal and make small steps toward achieving it. Lastly, we should learn to be truly happy. We should not look to others for happiness but ask God to put joy in our hearts. A good start would be to commit to eating healthy and letting go of destructive vices like excessive drinking, smoking, and gambling. God wants us to know that these things are just distractions that mask the pain that we have internally. We should also commit to doing and saying something nice to someone daily even if that means volunteering one's time. Being happy is a conscious decision and much like our walk with Christ, it takes effort and even if we stumble, we must dust ourselves off and try again.

## THINGS TO PONDER ON:

- Regardless of the criminal act that has been committed, God is forgiving. In order to move forward in one's life after acquiring a criminal record, it is paramount to start the forgiveness process. God gives many chances and the discipline was meant to be endured only for a season...........Hebrews 12:7-11

- Paul fought his flesh to keep it under subjection on a daily basis. He knew he had to stay away from people and activities that would cause him return to poor behavior. The same holds true for us. Paul's example tells us that it is a struggle at times to live a righteous life; however God has equipped us with the Holy Spirit to direct and speak to us and keep us out of trouble.............I Thessalonians 5:22

- Employees cannot impose their personal image in the workplace. Employees must adhere to dress code, code of ethics, and policy accordingly. The employer makes the rules and regulations to embody health and safety as well as unity for all. Perhaps, if one finds himself bucking the system on issues of tattoos, body piercings, and other personal imagery then it is time to reevaluate personal motives to see if one's personal values are in alignment with the company culture........ Genesis 1:27

- Workplace violence is repulsive, it never prompts goodness, it aims to destroy and victimize. What is your goal for the workplace? The Lord has plans for his children to prosper and reap a bountiful harvest from the efforts of the use of one's hands. Much too often, employees forget to do their job unto the Lord and completely remove the Lord from the equation of work. Employees must put the Lord first even while at work. Without a Godly focus workplace violence will come in like a flood. We must be willing to ask God to make us peacemakers.........Matthew 5:9

- Many seniors are forced to become semi-retired instead of relaxing, and enjoying life. Although, retirement is a goal for all workers it does not guarantee monetary stability for many. Primarily, we have to continue to plan for the stages of life with the admonishment of knowing God is our source who supplies every need completely. God promises he would not forsake us even in old age........ Psalms 37:25

- Are you ready to retire? Do you feel discouraged and fearful about retirement? Is your plan for retirement still on track? Has a major life-changing event interrupted your retirement plan? Upon answering these questions ask God to reveal any deficits and create a plan to close the gaps. A gap analysis would assist in benchmarking and devising realistic timelines to meet desired goals. The Lord promises in old age we would still bear fruit and flourish......Psalms 92:12-14

# INTERNAL WARRING

Everyone faces internal conflict when making tough decisions. This is actually a good thing . When we wrestle with making a tough decision, it shows that we are actually taking the matter seriously. However, it can become problematic when we stay stuck, remain indecisive, and fail to make a final decision. This situation happens constantly in the workplace. People are faced with making difficult decisions on a daily basis. Once more, what makes it even more complex is that most of these decisions will impact the employees in the work setting. No one ever said that making arduous decisions would be easy. There are several examples in the Bible of God having to make difficult decisions that He surely grappled with. In fact, when He decides to chastise us for our wrongdoing, it is as much as difficult for Him as it is for us because He loves us so much. God knows that making decisions is a hard task, which is why He wants to lead us every step of the way. Listening to God when making decisions requires us to listen to the Holy Spirit. In doing this, we are provided with rhema, or a spiritual word from Him. God lets us know that when we receive a rhema word from Him, we no longer have to have an internal war or conflict and we become confident in our decisions. It is only when we are not listening to His rhema word when we have internal conflict about making a decision. Some people are extremely indecisive with their decision making; particularly as it relates to work issues. It almost seems as if these type of people are going through a battle within their minds and spirits. For example, one minute the person can be completely confident in choosing a job in

137

another city and in the very next minute that person may have doubt. It is frustrating to see people go through these internal battles because God has an answer for them if they would just listen. Listening to a rhema word requires our spirit man to be stretched and pushed to places beyond what we have ever imagined. it requires us to meditate on His word daily, pray daily, and even cut some people out if they are speaking things into our lives contrary to what the Holy Spirit is telling us. One of the authors recalled having a friend whom had these internal battles; especially when it came to work issues. He would vacillate back and forth between the type of career that he wanted to have. In fact, this particular friend would often call the author and tell her that he has made up his mind about a particular field that he wanted to go into and then days later would tell her that he changed his mind. Undoubtedly, the author became extremely frustrated with this friend because she could not understand what was going on with him. Even further, he told her on several occasions that his family would actually talk him out of applying for a position or entering into a certain profession. She realized that this friend had an internal battle. Furthermore, it was revealed to her that he was listening to his family whom did not have his best interest in mind because he lacked the faith and discipline to listen to God to receive a rhema word. She also noticed that he would tell her that he was praying to God but continued to struggle with making decisions. What she realized is that he may have been praying to God but he might not have been filled with the Holy Spirit. To receive a rhema word, we must be filled with the Holy Spirit as evidenced by speaking in tongues. Many Christians, though faithful to God do not have the Holy Spirit which leaves them powerless. When we have the Holy Spirit in our spiritual arsenal, we develop the power to defeat Satan's attacks on our lives because we can talk to God in a "secret" language that the enemy cannot detect. Having the Holy Spirit is similar to when countries go to war and they communicate to one another in their native tongue. The enemy cannot decipher what they are saying because that is not their native language. Therefore, they can pass messages to one another about when and where to attack.

*Healing in the Workplace*

When making extremely difficult decisions that will impact the rest of our lives, we have to pray in tongues in order to receive a rhema word. Only then will we feel confident in our decisions no matter who may disagree because we will know that we truly have been in the presence of God's spirit.

## Scenario - BETTER YOU THAN ME:

*Cycom, Inc., is a corporation that sells computer software to local and regional companies. The office is devised of several sales teams and the goal is for each team member to make 25 sales per week. It is a high pressured job and the employees work under stressful conditions in an attempt to keep up with the sales quota. Joshua is one of the managers of one of the sales team and had manage fairly well over the past 3 years. His team tends to fall right in the middle when it comes to meeting the quota. Joshua supervisor has taken notice of this and would like for him to bring his teams numbers up. In fact, his supervisor has been putting an extreme amount of pressure on him by telling him that if his teams numbers are not brought up by the end of the quarter than he would be written up. Joshua was dismayed by this and asked his supervisor what more could he do to motivate his team. The supervisor snidely replied by saying "just make it happen". Joshua was ambivalent about putting an extreme amount of pressure on his team because he was not one to rule with an iron fist. However, he did not want to get written up and possibly lose his job. Joshua wrestle with this for days and finally told his team that if they did not pick up their numbers by the end of the week then they were going to get written up and lose overtime privileges. Joshua's team was confused by his sudden disposition. This was not the manager that they grew to admire and many of them thought about quitting the job all together.*

Pressure is a natural part of the workforce. We cannot escape the feeling of stress and pressure on our jobs. People whom expect that things will always be easy and smooth sailing without feeling some pressure actually have unrealistic views about the workplace. Often times, pressure and stress can be a good thing because it pushes us to grow and achieve things that we normally would not without the pressure. In fact, it can help build up our discipline, work ethic, and character. Only a foolish and childish person does not want to be pushed from time to time. Although receiving pressure and having some stress from our jobs can be a positive thing, it can also be problematic when the pressure and stress become too extreme. In some instances, this can occur when managers began to put an unrealistic amount of pressure on their employees. Most times, these unrealistic goals or overwhelming amount of pressure is placed on employees because managers are receiving the same thing from their bosses. For example, a manager might have to turn in a report to his supervisor and needs his staff to get their portion of the report done by a certain time. As the deadline approaches, this manager's boss may put some pressure on him to turn it in. As a result of him feeling pressured and stressed, he may pressure his staff to meet their requirements for the report. There is nothing wrong with managers operating like this; especially when the organization is depending upon the work to be completed. What is wrong; however is when managers exhibit tyrant-like behaviors and give out impractical demands just because they are feeling pressured. One way that managers can avoid behaving in such a way is to firmly, but sensitively talk to their staff about their expectations about meeting the goals of a task. Pastor Hokes said that he believes that in such cases, leaders need to bring their teams together and discuss issues without losing their poise. He also said that many leaders should practice the "sandwich technique" by first letting the staff know that their efforts are appreciated but they are moving to a time in which they all have to be pushed and the organization expects them to reach their goals at a much faster rate. He said that by doing this, the managers can be empathetic to the difficulties that the employees may be experiencing to complete their tasks in a timely fashion and the

*Healing in the Workplace*

employees can understand the manager's perspective without feeling pressured or becoming defensive. This is an effective strategy because it decreases putting a great deal of stress on employees, but it also gets the message across that they need to improve. Unfortunately for many managers, some employees will be resistant to this even when being approached about increasing their productivity in a respectful way. This actually suggests that these type of employees have a problem with authority and do not like others telling them what to do. Once more, when employees cannot handle constructive criticism about their work efforts, they are really communicating that they do not want to grow. Once more, they may be communicating that they do not want to grow within the organization and it suggests that they are not on board with the leader's vision of the project. Consider the example in the Bible of the man who gave talents, or money to his servants. In Matthew 25:14-29, the man dispersed talents to his servant two talents, and the last servant one talent. This man then went on a journey and left them. The first two servants took their talents and doubled them while the last servant took his talent and hid it in the ground. When the man returned he saw that the first two servants had doubled their talents and was pleased with their efforts. However, when he saw that the last servant took his talent and hid it in the ground, he called him lazy and wicked. God uses this example for many lessons but this can also be applied to employees whom have difficulty with their leaders pushing them to grow and expand their productivity efforts. Even though the man did not instruct his servants to double their talents, he did expect them to develop a plan that would help advance his vision. The last servant was called lazy and wicked because he did just hid the talent and walked away from his responsibility. When a leader gives an employee responsibilities to complete a task, it is that employees obligation to put in effort into completing that task. Once more, the employee has a duty to go above and beyond their usual efforts if they truly believe in the leader's vision. The last servant in the Bible was also called wicked because he walked away from his responsibility instead of attempting to work and please his lord. Employees whom have their own agenda

141

and do not follow their leader's instruction to complete a task are being wicked and devious. If we are given instructions to do something by our leader, then it is pleasing to God to put in every effort to meet the requirements. Once more, if we dismiss and minimize our manager's instructions, we are being haughty which is a spirit that is displeasing to God. First Lady Hokes said that some people just want to do what they want to do on the job instead of doing what their employers says to do. She also said that sometimes it is necessary to rule with an iron fist, much like Joshua in the vignette had to do. She reported that sometimes if managers do not supervise this way, then employees whom do not care about the organization's vision will steal company time and do their own thing. Managers must know how to cope with such employees and make them accountable for their productivity. Moreover, managers must know how to motivate and improve their employees productivity without allowing the pressure that they are receiving to threaten the relationship with their staff. One way that a manager could do this is by explaining to the staff that their productivity needs to be increased, per the organization's policy and then ask them what they are committed to doing to help meet this goal. First Lady Hokes said that Joshua or other managers can ask their team to verbalize what they believe that they can do to increase their workload. This helps because the employees are likely to feel like they are part of the solution instead of being the problem. Once more, managers can gather evidence from their employees about what is needed to help them improve and then take this information back to their supervisors to help the staff meet their goals. Pastor Hokes said that managers would be surprised to know that many employees fail to meet their tasks because they have not been equipped with all of the necessary items to complete the goal. For example, if employees need a specialized computer software to complete a task but the computer systems have been down for most of the day, this can gravely impact their productivity. It is the manager's responsibility to understand that this is an extenuating circumstance. Furthermore, employees are responsible in letting their supervisor's know about the problems that they are having to complete the task instead of hiding

*Healing in the Workplace*

it. Above all, the best things that managers can do in this situation is communicate effectively with their team, lead by example with their work ethic, stay firm with their expectations knowing that realistic demands helps their staff to grow, and involve them in creating the solutions to the problems.

## Scenario - BELIEF SYSTEM CHALLENGED WHEN MAKING DECISIONS:

*Ty Andrews is a retired musician turned entrepreneur and has developed commercial real estate all over the country. At an early age, Ty knew that he wanted to be a musician, a businessman, and give back to impoverished communities. He grew up in a low income part of town in Pennsylvania and his grandmother taught the spirit of giving. When Ty made his first million as a musician, he opened up a performing arts center in his home town to help cultivate the arts with inner city youth. Over the years, Ty has developed several youth centers and affordable housing for low income families. He is now working on a new idea to refurbish a poor community in Ohio. His ideas are to build a low cost Supermart, a new movie theater, and a fast food restaurant in this part of town. Ty was excited about this new project until his business partner, James told him that another commercial real estate developer had heard great things about him and wanted to partner with him and James to develop high rise apartment buildings in a more affluent area of Ohio. James told Ty that this potential partner would offer them a multimillion dollar deal to with them. Although, Ty was initially adamant about developing this poor city in Ohio, the multimillion dollar deal with this developer was enticing to him. He asked himself if he should stick to his beliefs of building up inner city communities even though it has been costly for him in the past or should he accept the multimillion deal.*

*L'Orangerie Crawford & Terri Harrison*

Our belief system is constantly being challenged as we face the issues of the world. This is especially hard for Christians because though we are not of the world, we are in it. Christians fall subject to sin because Satan always places situations in our lives to trip us up and tempt us. If we have struggled with using profanity before we became a Christian, Satan will manipulate situations that would tempt us to curse even when we are saved. If we struggled with drug use in the past, Satan will relentlessly make it hard for us to walk away from drugs even when we become Christians. The list goes on and on. Many Christians may question why they have fallen back into sin even after they faithfully follow God's principles and after they developed a strong belief system. The reason is, as Pastor Hokes explained that Satan is always after our testimony. He clarified that nonbelievers are looking to Christians to be the example in their lives and when we behave like them and engage in sin then Satan has stolen our testimony and we are no longer a viable witness to those nonbelievers whom have been watching us. This is why it is so important for us to hold on to our principles and beliefs because the work setting can be a hotbed of temptation and Satan is lurking around the corner to snatch our testimony away from us.

We all have belief systems. From the time that we are born into this world, our brains are sent messages that are coded into beliefs based upon what we witness in our environment. For example, if we have grown up in a household where our parents constantly fought, we are likely to develop a negative belief system about marriage. This belief system then can affect how we interact with our mates in adult relationships and may even dictate the type of relationships that we have. Some research has even suggested that we develop some beliefs based upon our learning environment in the womb. An example of this is if our mothers talk to us in a sweet voice while in the womb, we learn to recognize her voice and develop a belief that she is trustworthy. These two examples show that we all can and have developed negative and positive beliefs based upon our environment and experiences in life. The beliefs that we have are the foundation to our thinking. While most

*Healing in the Workplace*

people have positive thinking for most of the time, many people develop negative patterns of thinking that hinder their personal, educational, financial, occupational, or spiritual growth. This is why the word of God talks about having a renewal of the mind. This means that we not only have to renew our minds if our thoughts are negative, but we have to renew our beliefs. Simply put, we have to replace those negative beliefs with more positive beliefs through our behavior. How this happens is that we must change the way that we do things if it has negatively affected us in the past. That means that we have to walk away from the drugs and alcohol, and even let go of some people whom are not healthy for us in order to develop more positive beliefs. An example of this is that if we developed a negative belief about marriage based upon witnessing our parents argue, we may start to think about not getting married when we become an adult. To renew one's mind regarding this situation, one must start hanging around happy married couples and start developing alternative thinking that challenges that negative belief. Once more, it is equally important to decrease the amount of time one spends with single friends whom might be against marriage because this mindset just feeds into the negative belief about marriage. Some beliefs are necessary to get rid of otherwise we become limited in the way that we feel about ourselves and others in the world. However, some beliefs; especially Christians beliefs are essential to our survival in the world. It is crucial that we hold fast to our Christian principles in the workplace because God requires us to and because we are constantly being tempted with engaging in evildoings like extorting money from the company, tampering with important documents, or mistreating our colleagues. When we struggle internally with holding onto our principles, we likely have not developed a strong sense of self. We have to know who we are; particularly who we are in Christ to not compromise our beliefs when tempted to do so. Many Christians have heard about knowing who they are in Christ yet many of them do not actually know their "Christ-selves". The reason that they do not is because they have not turned to God's word to see what it says about them. God tells us who we are throughout the entire Bible. The problem

145

is that many Christians do not take the time to look at what the Bible says about them nor do they meditate on it and allow it to reach their heart. When we get our self-worth from what God says about us, we will start to develop Godly principles and beliefs and will not be faced with internal struggle when these beliefs are challenged. Pastor Hokes said that we have to be careful that we do not allow others; especially those with whom we are working to change our vision. If God has given us a clear vision, we must go with what He says no matter how much our colleagues or partners oppose. Once more, he said that we have to revisit our vision every 26 to 30 days to ensure that the vision stays on course with our Godly principles and beliefs and not with worldly beliefs. Ty in the vignette was having an internal battle between making money and building up low income communities. If Ty had received a vision from God to continue refurbishing downtrodden communities and this belief was instilled in him from God, then he has a duty to see it through. God wants us to know that He will never give us a vision that is not built on His principles and beliefs. In addition, He will never put a vision in our hearts before its due time. First Lady Hokes said that timing is everything when making a difficult decision. She said that Ty needed to listen to God about the timing for both of the projects. Additionally, she said that when faced with making difficult decisions we must adhere to the word of God and deliberate on the scripture in 1 Corinthians 10:23. In the scripture, Paul writes that all things are lawful but not expedient which means that all things are permissible but not advantageous. Just because an opportunity seems beneficial does not mean that God wants us to jump at it. It may not be the right time or it may not be in conjunction with our Godly principles and beliefs. We as Christians have to be careful to not let anyone or anything sway us from what we know to be right. Some of our colleagues can have a crafty way of alluring us into evildoing, but we must know who we are in Christ and stay true to our beliefs. When we know that we have made the right decision based on Godly beliefs, then there is no one who can manipulate us. Besides, God's word says that if He is for us then who can be against us?

*Healing in the Workplace*

## Scenario - SPEAKING OUT AGAINST INAPPROPRIATENESS:

*Kyle is a claims adjuster and he likes his job. He seems to get alone with almost everyone in the office; particularly because he likes to appease them. Kyle has a way of changing who he is to fit the group that he is in for that moment. Once he is done socializing then he is back to being himself. He particularly likes to hang around a group that is considered to be troublemakers. He likes them because they are exciting and funny and he likes to be considered the sensible one out of the group. One day, one of these troublemakers harassed another worker and even outright bullied him. Kyle had witnessed this on several occasions. The bullied employee eventually complained to the office manager who then investigated the incident. The bullied employee identified Kyle as a witness. Kyle was asked by the office manager to discuss his side of the story. Kyle lied to her and told her that he did not see nor hear anything. He decided to not speak out against his friends' inappropriate behavior out of fear of being disliked and ostracized from the group. Since there was a lack of evidence, the office manager was forced to give the bully a warning but the bullied employee felt slighted.*

Speaking up for others' rights and speaking out against inappropriate behaviors at work is another thing that causes internal conflict. When we witness our colleagues misbehaving, many of us have an unsettled feeling in the pit of our stomachs. For Christians, this unsettled feeling is us being convicted by our Godly principles, knowing that what we are witnessing is wrong. Some of us adhere to this feeling and decide to speak out against inappropriateness in the office while others may ignore it and not want to get involved. God holds us just as accountable as the offender if we intentionally disengage ourselves and decide to overlook our colleagues' transgressions.

There are many motives for not speaking out against inappropriate behavior at work when we know that the offender(s) is wrong. One of the reasons as shown in the vignette is the failure to know oneself. Kyle did not know who he was and attempted to please everyone even at the expense of refusing to speak out against his friend's bully behavior. Some people whom fail to tell others when they are wrong and overlook their misbehaviors do so because they themselves do not know whom they are. Once more, if they do not know whom they are, how could they possibly tell someone else whom they should be? People whom speak out against wrongdoings are confident because they know whom they are and they believe in their principles. They do not have to shape themselves into other people's view of whom they should be because they have been shaped by God. Pastor Hokes said that we need to allow God to shape and mold us into what He wants us to be and not be everything to everyone. In Jeremiah 18:1-6, Pastor Hokes explained that God tells us that He wants to shape us like the potter shapes the clay. When we allow God to place His hands on our lives, He will mold us into confident people whom stand by their principles and rebuke the wrongdoings of others, even if the wrongdoers are our friends. Once more, god wants us to know that if we fail to tell our colleagues, even when they are our friends when they are wrong then we really do not care about them. Pastor Hokes suggested that Kyle in the vignette did not know himself which is why he was behaving like a chameleon and attempting to fit in with everyone on his job. He also suggested that he may have not been affirmed as a young child by his parents or other significant adults in his life, which is why he never grew into knowing himself. Pastor Hokes said that this is why it is so important for fathers; especially fathers of young boys to remain active in their lives. He said that it is only in the presence of other men when boys will become men. He also said that even if fathers are not in the household and children are being raised by their mothers, children still need to be given self-worth, otherwise they will grow up being influenced by everyone except for being influenced by God. When we are influenced by God, we do not have to wrestle with a decision

*Healing in the Workplace*

to speak up for what is right because He has given us the self-worth and confidence to do so. Moreover, we must be confident to speak out against transgressions at work even if we risk persecution. God clearly tells us in His word that we pay a price when we follow Him. He never said that we would not go up against persecution and in fact, He wants us to expect persecution from others when we adhere to His principles. What He does want us to know is that we mustn't be afraid because He will never leave us when we stay faithful to Him. When we are faced with speaking out against someone's wrongdoing at work, we have to be as courageous as David was when he fought Goliath. David was not afraid of Goliath even though the other Israelites were afraid because David knew who he was. More importantly, David was confident in the God that he served and knew that God has his back. When we are confident in ourselves and confident in God protecting us, we do not have to be afraid of any potential harm if we rebuke the bad behavior of others. Furthermore, we do not have to comply with others for the fear of being disliked. Pastor Hokes said that people like Kyle whom behave differently depending upon their setting and fail to be whom they really are out of fear of being disliked are really "wannabes". God wants us to stop being "wannabes" and be the people that He called us to be. When we finally become who He wants us to be, we will have the power and confidence to tell others when they are wrong. Once more, we will have the confidence to convict ourselves when we are wrong. We must be able to rebuke our own misbehaviors and right our wrongs. First Lady Hokes said that Kyle could have made amends with the employee who was bullied by apologizing for not speaking up for what is right. When we fail to right our wrongs and apologize for our mistakes, we are being prideful and showing a lack of empathy for other people's feelings. Once more, when we fail to apologize, we are caring more about being right and having the upper hand. God's word tells us in James 5:16 that we must confess our sins to one another so that we may be healed. The affects of apologizing for our wrong doings can be rewarding for our relationships. It can stop an argument from going on too long unnecessarily and it can heal both the victim and the

149

offender. Once more, it helps to build one's character. God needs us to be courageous and speak out against inappropriateness, even if done by our friends or if we are the offender. He needs us to do so because He needs brave and just people in His army.

## THINGS TO PONDER ON:

- Too often, employees forget managers have a difficult position to be in. They have to please upper management all while pleasing their staff. God is faithful to his people at all times especially when it might not seem so favorable to man. Showing lack of support to managers is ungodly in the eyes of God while it breeds dissension amongst staff and must be immediately put under subjection............Roman 16:17-18

- Stop and think about a time at work when a situation happened where the supervisor gathered all the team together to discuss a task. Was anyone there who actually tried to put a damper on the project with their negative attitude or snide remarks? Have you ever been the one who talked to another employee about management in a non supportive manner? Paul cautioned the church to be careful in spreading spiteful talk and rumors about leadership as it is an act of disrespect and foolishness. Jude expresses if we participate in spreading division we are lusting after our own ungodly worldliness.........Jude 18, 19

- Deciding to go into business with another person has its challenges, but for the most part it renders great rewards. Partners do not see eye-to-eye on all aspects of business. However, they are smart to talk out their differences before it turns into problematic situations. Consider Noah when God told him to build the Ark he knew in his spirit God spoke to him and he did not deviate from his belief. Noah's business

*Healing in the Workplace*

partners were his entire family who at first may have thought him to be a bit eccentric but thankfully he held his ground and did not sway from his plan to construct the Ark. Noah's faith proved to stand the test of time........Hebrews 11:7

- When David went to battle he always took trustworthy partners with him. David understood battle and his reputation preceded him throughout the nation. The Bible tells us in the book of Mark that David was considerate not just of himself during battle but of the well-being of his soldiers as well. He even went as far as entering into unforbidden territory of the high priest Abiathar to comfort his troops. True partnership shows consideration, trustworthiness, and respect........Mark 2:25-26

- It takes a strong person to stand up for what is right; especially in the workplace. The Lord requires that we are our brothers' keeper and we must speak against even our brother if he is committing inappropriate acts. The Lord did not create us to be cowards, timid, nor fearful. What have you chosen to overlook out of fear of not being accepted by the so called "in crowd"?.........2 Timothy 1:7

- There is a saying that if you don't stand up you will stand for anything. Do you see inappropriate behavior in the workplace and sit back and say nothing? What type of inappropriate behavior have you witnessed at work and turned your eye because you did not want to get involved? How many times has God nudged you to speak up regarding workplace inappropriateness but you continued to keep quiet? In the book of Ezekiel God tells the prophet to speak up and warn the Israelites of their bad behavior or they would surely die.........Ezekiel 3

# -ISM'S IN THE WORKPLACE

Many people may not be aware that anti-discriminatory laws for the workplace has been in place since the early 1960s. In fact, the civil rights movement was the catalyst for the implementation of equal opportunities for all. According to Title VII of the Civil Rights Act of 1964, employers are prohibited to discriminate against any prospective candidate or employee because of race, religion, sexual orientation, or creed. The Equal Employment Opportunity Commission (EEOC) is the agency that enforces this law. Though this law ensures the protection of employees, several organizations continue to discriminate against them. Some organizations discriminate in more covert ways by asking inappropriate questions while others overtly discriminate by refusing to hire certain employees because of their race, age, sexual orientation, or religion. Some of the inappropriate questions that many recruiting and hiring managers are not aware that they cannot ask during an interview are asking about a candidate's marital status or whether or not the candidate has children. There are many more questions that are not to be asked during an interview. The bottom line is that there are hidden discriminatory messages in asking these forbidden questions which is why the law is in place to protect us. Discrimination certainly does not exist only in the workplace, but given that many of us spend most of our time in the work environment, it is likely that most if not all of us will experience discrimination at some point in our lives. Discrimination,

*Healing in the Workplace*

though a natural occurrence of life, can be devastating to the soul. It causes people to doubt themselves, their worth, and their place in society. Discrimination of all types is distressing. However, many have argued that racism is the most dreadful form of discrimination that has been entrenched in American History. Just thinking about America's history regarding race relations can bring tears to anyone's eyes. Our ancestors, whether of European or African descent fought tirelessly for equal opportunities in America, yet America has not always been the land of opportunity. Far too often, limitations have been placed on people because of their race that has led to detrimental effects. One can look at any "ghetto" across America and see the negative impact of racism. Discrimination against others is not only restricted to American History. The truth is that discrimination is a long standing problem that has been in existence since the beginning of time. Throughout the Bible, discrimination is a topic of concern and God gives us guidelines on how to cope with it. One of the greatest examples of discrimination in the Bible is when Jesus was gathering His disciples and Philip found Nathanael. Philip told Nathanael that Jesus was the Messiah that Moses wrote about in the laws, but Nathanael appeared to be unimpressed. In fact, he asked Philip if anything good can come out of Nazareth? Nathanael was discriminating against Jesus because of his perception of how people from Nazareth behaved. Philip challenged Nathanael by telling him to "come and see". Philip instructed Nathanael to meet Jesus because he wanted him to learn Jesus' character rather than judging Him because of where He was born. This example shows that we all have our own prejudices against others based on our observations, experiences, and the things that we have been taught as children. However, the most powerful part about this example is that God wants us to be like Philip and challenge ourselves and others to reexamine our prejudices by getting to know others' character before we judge them. God wants us to do the same in the work setting. He wants all of us to be aware of our prejudices and keep them in check and challenge ourselves to get to know one another's heart despite the differences. If Nathanael had not taken Philip's challenge to meet Jesus and learn about His character, he would have missed out on an opportunity to follow and study under the Son of Man. God does not want us to miss out on working with great people because we are allowing our prejudices to get in the way.

## Scenario - AGE-ISM:

*Marlene has just been promoted to an associate director position in a nonprofit that provides shelter to homeless youth. She is extremely Knowledgeable and holds a Masters Degree in Social Work. Her only problem, or so says the other employees is that she's very young, 25 years old to be exact. Because of her age and youthful appearance, she is rarely taken seriously by some of the seasoned directors. During program development meetings she usually comes in with innovative ideas but is overlooked and dismissed because many feel that she has not worked in the field long enough to give directives. Peter is having a different issue regarding his age on his job as a human resources specialist at a toy manufacturing company. He is a very competent worker and rarely misses a day from work. He has been at this job for 17 years now and is seeking a human resources manager position to increase his skills set. The human resources director; however is more keen on hiring a younger person to fill the position because she is fearful that Peter just does not have the energy to keep up with work demands. AST Industries has a lively group of employees working for the company; many of the employees are friends and socialize with one another on weekends away from their job duties. The office however seems to be divided not among men and women, not among manager and subordinates, but among the "young and old". The younger employees tend to go lunch together and the older employees often sit by one another during meetings. Even the employees themselves have noticed this divide and they just chalk it up as the culture of the company.*

*Healing in the Workplace*

There is an interesting phenomenon that is occurring in the world today. Technology and modern science have given people the opportunity to live longer than ever before. This means that people are healthy enough to work well into their seventies. Because of this, multiple generations are represented in the workplace. The Baby Boomers, Generation X-ers, and Millennials, or Generation Y-ers are now working together in organizations. Due to the generational differences, conflict often occurs because one generation sees and does things differently than the next. As a result, ageism is likely to occur. One of the reasons why these generations cannot get along in the workplace is because neither one is valuing the input of the other. Once more, the different generations undermine the skills that the other has to offer to the workforce. The devaluing of other generations is sinful because God wants us all to respect one another and what we have to offer. The Bible actually gives several examples of the conflict that can arise as a result of the generational gap. The differences between King David and his family is a prime example of generational differences. David was the first generation who led the Israelites and had a clear vision given to him by God. However, when Solomon, David's son ruled, he rebelled against his father's vision and it led to the Israelites' struggle between worshipping God or Ba'al, or a false god. Rehoboam was Solomon's son and also reigned over the Israelites. Unlike his grandfather and father, he did not have a vision at all and often waivered in his commitment to God. Rehoboam's leadership ultimately contributed to a division between the Israelites whom followed God and those whom did not. This type of situation is frequently played out in the workplace because the generations' visions are not on one accord. It is organizations' responsibility to bridge the generational gap and help everyone have the same vision. One of the ways in which an organization can do this is by helping each employee to see the value that the other brings to the organization. Organizations can create a policy that has the various generations teach one another about the specifics of their job duties. For example, Baby Boomers are likely to have more knowledge and more experience about tasks because of their age while Generation Y-ers are likely to have more knowledge about technology. Baby Boomers can teach the Generation Y-ers about the "ins and outs" of the workplace while Generation Y-ers can teach the Baby Boomers about computers. This could be a perfect formula for building camaraderie amongst the generations. Unfortunately, many employees still may not be open to such a policy because of their own stubbornness. Pastor Hokes said that he has seen this issue in the church where many of the youth lack the desire to learn from the older church members. He said that many older churchgoers want to and have reached out to the younger members to give them guidance, but they are often shunned by them. He said that God revealed to him that today's generation is a generation that does not like authority nor do they value the wisdom of the older adults. Pastor Hokes recalled being a teenager and yearning his father's wisdom about life and work experiences. He said that today's youth have lost the longing to sit at the elders feet and listen to them. First Lady Hokes said that young people need the older generation because they have yet to acquire wisdom and experience. She also said that younger employees need to acknowledge that the older employees still can have the drive to accomplish tasks at work. In fact, she reported that the Bible states that Moses was 80 years old when he worked to lead the children of Israel out of Egypt. Pastor Hokes said that we have to be careful to not shut out the seasoned employees. This can have negative implications both legally and interpersonally. Though respecting the views of older employees is necessary for the growth of teams in organizations, it is also important that employees value the knowledge of the younger generations. For example, Marlene in the vignette was not valued by her colleagues because she was younger. This could have created a disharmony among the teach with which she was working. God tells us to value the young just as much as we are to value the old. In Matthew 21:12-16, the Bible talks about valuing the words from children. In the scriptures, Jesus went to the temple and was displeased with what He saw. He declared that the temple be a house of prayer and not a house of thieves and when the children saw this, they cried out and praised Him. However, the chief priest and scribes were offended and asked Jesus if He heard

*Healing in the Workplace*

what the children were saying? When Jesus answered, He told them that out of the mouths of babes, praise is perfected. Jesus is suggesting in this scripture that there is an innocence in young people that should be valued among the old. The youth are yet to be jaded with the ways of the world and this should be cherished by others; particularly in the workplace. Even further, younger employees tend to have a vibrant and enthusiastic spirit that can rub off on the older employees. God is displeased when He sees a divide between generations; especially in the workplace because He calls all of us to work together for His purpose. First Lady Hokes said that all generations should complement one another in the workplace. Moreover, Pastor Hokes said that the balance between generations is shown in the Old and New Testaments of the Bible. He said that some ministers only preach the gospel from the Old or the New Testaments, but what they fail to remember is that God created both Testaments for a purpose. He said that the Old Testament is the foundation leading up to the New Testament. In addition, he reported that we must not forget that Jesus was prophesied in the Old Testament which suggests that it was written for a purpose. God wants us to get to a point where we appreciate one another in the workplace regardless of age. He wants us to welcome the differences in experiences that we have from one another and embrace the various skills that we bring to the table. First Lady Hokes suggested that employers give accolades for the various differences such as praising an employee for his or her computer skills while praising another for his or her customer service and communicative skills. By doing this, a precedence can be set for the employees to praise one another for their differences. God does not want us to put a divide between the young and the old. He wants us to know that He is there for us all. In 1 John 2:12-12, God says that He has written to us all: The children, the fathers, and the young men. He tells us in His word that He does not love one generation more than the other. Therefore, we have to be like Him and love one another equally regardless of our age differences.

157

*L'Orangerie Crawford & Terri Harrison*

## Scenario - RACE-ISM:

*Charles works for an electronics store in Los Angeles. He is Native American and represents his tribe proudly. He is always educating some of the other employees on Native American customs and traditions and he has even brought in some Native American cuisine for some employees to taste. Raquel is a newly hired employee at the same electronics store and she is also Native American but from a different tribe than Charles. Charles has a disdain for Raquel's tribe and has frequently gives her dirty looks when she passes by or refuses to help her when she asks him questions. He also likes going to his colleagues to tell them how much Raquel's tribe is beneath him and how his tribe has a history of warriors while hers are low-lives, drunks, and thieves. He also refers to them as "those people" and says that Raquel's tribe makes Native Americans look bad. This has seriously affected the dynamic of the office because some of the other employees have become uncomfortable with Charles' negative comments about Raquel's tribe.*

Racism is still a taboo issue; especially as it relates to the workplace. It can come in many forms such as racial slurs, comments, or inferences about one's race. It can also be the unfair treatment of others such as withholding vital work information because of race. It can even occur in the form of stereotyping. Some people do not realize that there are both negative and positive stereotypes that can still be racist. For example, we certainly know that inferring that a particular race is inferior is negative. If an individual believes that African Americans have inferior intelligence, this is a negative stereotype. However, making a stereotype based on a positive quality is also racist. An example of this is suggesting that all Asian Americans are good in math. Although it is a wonderful thing to be great at math, it is racist to assume that all Asian Americans possess this attribute. We know that it is illegal to overtly discriminate against someone in the workplace because of race. In actuality, it is much easier to build a case against an employer or

*Healing in the Workplace*

colleague if the discrimination is obvious. However, many people do not know what to do when the discrimination is more covert, like being a victim to positive stereotyping. God can help us cope with these type of incidences. God instructs us how to stop racism in its tract if we just follow what He tells us.

The Bible gives an account of various occurrences that can explain the root of racism. God loves us all and does not favor one race over the other. Many may question this since the Jews are the chosen people. However, the Bible tells us in the New Testament that Jesus was sent to save us all. Even Peter spoke this word to the Gentiles to save them from sin. In Galatians 3:8, the Bible says that God would justify the Gentiles by faith. Even further, Galatians 3:28-29 says that neither Jew nor Greek is favored, but we are all one in Christ Jesus and if we belong to Him then we are all seeds of Abraham. Since God loves us all regardless of our race, the question still remains: why is there still racism? The answer is more complex than anyone would ever imagine. Many economists believe that racism still exists because there remains a competition for scarce goods, while the psychological view is that racist views have been passed down generationally within families. Regardless of which perspective is right, the underlying issue is that people continue to engage in racist practices and have racist beliefs because of the lack of acceptance for the differences between groups. Pastor Hokes said that before we judge one another because of race, we must do some research on the differences between the races. He said that we may grow to understand and appreciate the differences. Ethnic differences between the Jews and Samaritans are well documented in the Bible. The two groups had long standing hostility toward one another. One of the reasons of the hate is because after the Jews fell to the Assyrian empire, they began to intermarry. The Samaritans were the result of the intermarriage and were considered to be "half-breeds" and not of a pure race. Even though the Samaritans were considered to be un-pure, they were known as one of the largest followers of God's teachings. This shows us that God can redeem us and turn around what people think is "unclean" for His will. For example, Charles in the vignette thought that he was better than Raquel because her tribe has a history of thieves and drunks. Even if this was true, God could have used Raquel to change Charles' mind about her tribe by showing him the goodness in her. Charles was out of line and disrespectful to Raquel. Pastor Hokes said that he needed to humble himself and not think that he was better than her. He also said that in Romans 12:3, God tells us that no man shall think too highly of himself, but must think soberly. This suggests that anyone who thinks too highly of him or herself is immature because they are ignorant to God's word. Charles' actions toward Raquel were immature and could have resulted in severe disciplinary action toward him. First Lady Hokes reported that Charles or people whom are racist like him need to be dealt with by their employers. She said that things like this should not be taken lightly. One of the things that victims of racism in the work environment can do is to address the concern with the offender's supervisor. Victims can also anonymously call the internal hotline to make a complaint. In addition, the injured party can utilize his or her local union and get the EEOC involved to investigate the matter. This should only be the last resort if the racist acts are not being dealt with by the offender's supervisor. Once more, people must not be quick to declare racism before they examine the entire situation. In fact, Pastor Hokes said that we mustn't walk around with the race card in our pockets. Instead, we must first see if we are misconstruing the situation and get clarification if we are unsure that something our colleague is saying is racist. This is especially necessary for more covert forms of racism. The offenders of racism also need help. One of the things that they desperately need is cultural diversity training. Organizations have a responsibility to send all employees to diversity and sensitivity trainings since the workplace is become more and more diverse. Offenders also need to be aware of their prejudices and learn to keep them in check by limiting what they say about other ethnic groups while at work. Even further, they can learn to be more tolerant by challenging themselves to learn more about other people's culture before they judge them based off of what they have heard or seen in the media. God does not want us

*Healing in the Workplace*

to compare ourselves to one another, as said by First Lady Hokes. She said that Paul states in 2 Corinthians 10:12 that it is unwise to measure ourselves against one another. There is no room to compare ourselves in God's kingdom because He sees us as the same and loves us equally.

## SEX-ISM:

*Martin is a successful and talented graphics designer at Webbie Designs, LLC. For the past year, he has been transforming himself from a man to a woman. He believed that he was born a woman in a man's body as early as he could remember and he was just now feeling confident enough to get gender reassignment surgery. His transformation was subtle in the beginning and he thought that doing it this way would help his coworkers adjust. He eventually got the surgery and came to work a few weeks later, now as Shannon. Shannon dressed like a woman, and behaved like a woman. She even started to use the women's bathroom. The male employees began vocalizing their disgust with Shannon and went to senior management to make complaints on how her appearance is a distraction from them doing their job. The women ostracized Shannon and would not speak to her. One woman even asked her why she was using the women's bathroom and said that it made her feel uncomfortable. Shannon was so hurt by the way her colleagues treated her. They could not believe that the same people whom respected her when she was Martin could loathe her as Shannon. She became depressed and could no longer do her job. She was eventually placed on disability and had to undergo psychiatric treatment for her depression.*

Sexist behavior is nothing new in the workplace. For years, women have been the brunt of crude comments and outright sexual harassment. These type of behaviors suggest a negative attitude toward women. In today's society, there are various forms of sexism that go beyond sexual advances. Sexism can be the mistreatment of someone because

161

of his or her gender or excluding someone from the group because of gender. This form of sexism is harder to prove because people can make other excuses for why they have excluded a colleague. For example, if a woman working on a predominantly male team is excluded from a project, it would be difficult for her to prove that it is because of her gender because they can claim that she has a harsh personality, or that she does not produce high quality work. It would be up to her to prove that they are making these claims because of her gender. This type of manipulation reminds us that Satan's devices are subtle. He finds ways to make us believe that we are imagining things or that we really are incompetent when there is likely to be real discrimination happening to us. God does not want us to be deceived. We must recognize the warning signs so that we would not become victim to Satan's plan to destroy us.

Many people do not realize that both men and women can experience sexism. The term is actually defined as any discriminatory actions or beliefs toward persons because if their gender. The results of sexism can be damaging to both the victim and the perpetrator. The victim can begin to doubt his or her abilities and worth in the organization while the offender can be sued and even terminated from the job. We must all learn to deal with one another's gender differences even if it makes us feel uncomfortable because God instructs us to respect one another. We all know that the Bible discusses gender roles but many people do not know what it says about dealing with gender issues. The Bible famously recounts Deborah who judged over Israel. Though she was a women, she was revered by many. Even Barak, a male warrior who was commanded by Deborah gather the tribes to go to Mount Tabor, respected her and would not go unless she went with him. God gives us this example to show us that women and men should respect one another's leadership in the workplace, yet many of us continue to struggle with this. Even further, we must respect one another regardless of one's sexual orientation or identification. For instance, Martin who slowly transformed himself into Shannon in the vignette was mistreated

*Healing in the Workplace*

by his colleagues. Many of them found it uncomfortable to work with him because he now identified with being a woman. Though God is not pleased with Shannon's choice given that He tells us that He made no mistakes when He made us, He is equally displeased with Shannon's colleagues' behavior toward her. Pastor Hokes said that we do not have to like nor condone the act of homosexuality, but we are not to mistreat these individuals either. He said that we must be longsuffering with people like Shannon whom have changed their sexual identity and treat her the same as if she was Martin. However, Pastor Hokes makes it clear that from a spiritual perspective, Shannon's actions should not be overlooked. In fact, both he and First Lady Hokes said that Shannon should have prepared herself for her colleagues being uncomfortable especially since she started going into the women's bathroom. Pastor Hokes said that Shannon has changed her natural image and professed to God that He made a mistake when He made her as a man. Pastor Hokes said that the spirit that Shannon has over her is a deceiving and lustful spirit. In fact, in 1 Timothy 4:1, the Bible tells us that in the latter days, many will depart from the faith and heed to deceiving spirits and doctrine. One of the most deceitful doctrines that Satan could ever tell someone is that who God made them was a mistake. God does not make mistakes. He knows us before we even know ourselves. He knows these things because He has already mapped out our lives before we are born. What limits and hinders us from accomplishing His will is our own lustfulness. First Lady Hokes said that deceitful spirits come upon us because we are lustful with our flesh. Furthermore, Pastor Hokes gave an example of how we allow lust to come into our hearts and deceive us. He said that everything usually starts with looking at an enticing object. He said to think about a man who sees a woman's body part whether it be in a pornographic image or during his daily routine. He said that because men are visual beings, it is often enticing to them to see a woman's body. He then said that if this man is married and does not shield himself from those images, when he goes home, he is no longer interested in his wife because his flesh has already been fed by looking at the enticing images. Once more, if this man

163

continues to feed his flesh by looking at seductive images, then he can become susceptible to developing deceitful spirits like adultery. From a spiritual viewpoint, this is exactly what happened to Shannon and other transgender individuals. The more they fed their spirits with Satan's lies that they were not good enough the way God made them, the more they were vulnerable to a deceptive spirit. Although God does not condone changing one's sex, He wants others to respect them because they are still His children. God still wants us to be professional while at work and show His love to them through us. Furthermore, we will never be able to witness to them if we shut them out because of our unpleasant feelings about their choices.

## THINGS TO PONDER ON:

- God is so exact and deliberate in his creations. When he created man in the image and likeness of him he created man to have the ability to walk in love towards one another and to respect hierarchy amongst the generations. For example, the elderly are to guide the young through teachable moments under the admonishment of Godly principles. Also, he tells us to have love and respect for the aging and recognize the importance of old and young growing together. When the young shows contempt for the old it is disgraceful as well it is a dangerous act. God tells us he will not tolerate being prideful and we are to quickly repent for such behavior. Today, do yourself a favor ask yourself who do you have contempt for because of their age (old or young)? Be swift to repent as delayed action is linked to direct disobedience............I Peter 5:1-4 NKJV

- It is terrible to witness disrespect but to be on the receiving end seems much worst. Imagine being an older person trying to interact with a younger person or group but they do not want you around or cannot receive any instruction from you because

*Healing in the Workplace*

of your age. Have you been the deliverer or the receiver of such action? If so, ask for forgiveness and give the gift of forgiveness this is extremely powerful. God instructs we are to honor our elders and fear him; and we are to honor our parents.....Lev 3, 19 NKJV

- Racism is showing partiality towards others which is against the Lord. No one is greater or better than the other which is why it is deemed as hatred. While man may find it fitting to think it appropriate to judge others based on preconceived notions it is unacceptable to our Lord. The Lord tells us in First John, James, and Romans that we are to not hate our brother, not to show partiality, and God is not partial. We must always check ourselves first before we begin to think it proper to judge someone else.......I John 2:9, James 2:9, Romans 2:11 NKJV

- The Lord is the world's example of true leadership. He does not show partiality, he is no respect of person, he is nonthreatening, and he is all inclusive of others. If you are a manager or aspire to become a manager do you possess the same qualities the Lord has in leading us in our daily lives? True leadership starts with modeling the very leadership qualities of our Lord. Do a self-evaluation pertaining to what leadership qualities you have or may be lacking. Whatever the outcome do not be upset if it is not so favorable; instead accept the challenge to partner with the Lord and allow the reflection of his qualities to manifest...... Ephesians 6:9 NKJV

- Have you ever thought about what the Lord says regarding sexism? The bible tells us in Galatians there is no division of people, that we are all one in Christ Jesus. Further, there is no place for separatism. Sexism is expressed in different ways, can you identify a sexiest? Moreover, are you a sexiest? Ask

*L'Orangerie Crawford & Terri Harrison*

for deliverance if you struggle with this spirit of division.......
Galatians 3:28 NKJV

- Although the word tells us woman was made for man, it does not give a man the right to think he can dominate over the woman. Being sexiest usually comes across as domineering which has a host of underlining attitudes and behaviors that violate personal space of others. In the workplace respect for a fellow coworker is mandatory whether we agree or disagree with their lifestyle. No one has a right to bash, name call, or snarl at anyone in the workplace if sudden transformations occur appearance wise to a fellow coworker. God expects us to remain respectful and prayerful at all times. Do not encourage acts of hatred or sexism instead repel those who enforce this deliberate mindset. Perhaps, you may work with someone exhibiting sexiest characteristics and you feel the need to address it; take the opportunity to share with them the wonderful qualities they have that are being overshadowed by sexism..........I Corinthians 11:9 NKJV

# MANAGING CONFLICT

Organizations spend an endless amount of money seeking professional guidance to manage conflict in the workplace. Conflict can be one of the most damaging issues in a work setting because it often leads to a whole host of problems, including but not limited to poor performance, high employee turnover, and even physical and verbal altercations. Although conflict can become problematic, it is a natural part of life. There are so many different personality types in the world, and differing of opinions that it is inevitable that conflict will arise from time to time. Conflict between people can actually be a healthy thing because it can be a sign of growth in the relationship and/or growth of an individual in the relationship. For example, imagine a couple that has been together for several years and one of them wants to go back to college. The other person may feel threatened because of their partner's decision to grow and this tension may cause conflict. In this case, it may not be a negative thing that the couple is having some conflict. One of the reasons why the couple may be having the conflict is because the person who is threatened by the partner's decision to go back to school may just need some reassurance that his or her needs will still get met. Additionally, the individual who wants to go back to school may feel some tension because they feel unsupported by the other partner. Both of the partner's feelings are equally as important and can actually serve as an opportunity for them to grow with one another if handled properly. The problem that arises with conflict is that it is hardly ever handled appropriately by either party involved. Most times,

167

we have valid reasons for feeling a certain way in a relationship but do a poor job at communicating these concerns. Instead of communicating our concerns in a non-threatening way, we often make the mistake of communicating our feelings by threatening, screaming, stonewalling or refusing to answer questions, becoming defensive, and ignoring the other person altogether. The list goes on and on and we all have been guilty of communicating our feelings this way to others at some point in our lives. When both members of the relationship communicate in this manner is when conflict occurs. God wants us in any relationship that we are in whether it be in mother-daughter, husband-wife, or colleague-supervisor to stop viewing tension as a negative thing and understand that it can be used as an opportunity to grow in the relationship together. It is a known fact in research that people bond the most when there is tension and adrenaline. This is why most relationship experts advise couples to do something adventurous together like go hiking, bungee jumping, or skydiving because the adrenaline and tension that it causes creates an automatic bond between them. When the couple engages in these type of activities, hormones are flowing throughout their brains and it tells them that if they can get through this scary and exhilarating experience together, then they can get through anything together. Once more, after the experience is over, the couple is more likely to trust one another because of what they just have gone through together. This is how God actually views conflict. He knows that frightening experiences and events will come our way. He also knows that there are many things that will happen in our relationships with others that will threaten us. However, He wants us to use these experiences to bond with the other person and trust that He will see us through. If we start to trust that He will get us through the conflict in our relationships, then we will start to trust the other person even more. When we have conflict in our relationships with others, God wants us to remember the scripture in James 1:2-3 that states that we should be joyful when we have trials and tribulations because it is a test of our faith and it produces patience. This scripture is so poignant; particularly when we think about the relationship that we have with our family, friends, and

*Healing in the Workplace*

colleagues because it is telling us that instead of feeling threatened when we have conflict with them, be joyful because we can use the conflict to trust and become more patient with one another. The problem; however with this is that many of us have issues with trust. Some of us have a difficult time trusting others because of what we experienced in our childhood, while some of us learn to not trust others because we have been burned in past relationships. We have to remember that trust is at the core of any healthy relationship and if we cannot trust others then our relationships are doomed to fail. No one is saying that it is easy to trust. In fact, it may be the hardest thing that we have to do because it means that we have to be vulnerable and unguarded. Many Christians may even use scriptures in the Bible to support their lack of trust in other people. For example, some scriptures like Psalms 118:8 state that it is better to trust in the Lord than to trust in man. This scripture is not suggesting that we should not trust in other people. What it is really suggesting is that we should not worship other people. Sometimes we can love, cherish, and put all of our trust in people with whom we have a relationship so much that we begin to worship them. We cannot worship others because people are without fault. We have to remember that anything worthy of being worshipped is without any flaws and fault. Often times, we become disappointed and let down by those with whom we have a relationship because we worship them and forget that they have their own flaws and issues that they bring into the relationship. This ten causes conflict; however, we must remember that the only being that is perfect and that cannot disappoint us, thus worthy of being worshipped is God. If we can remember that none of us are perfect and will disappoint the ones we love and are closest to from time to time, then we can better prepare ourselves when conflict arises.

## EMPLOYEE/SUPERVISOR CONFLICT:

Myrna is a manager at a local coffee shop. She has three barista employees under her management, all of whom are afraid to confront her on her inappropriate and harsh communication skills toward them. She frequently puts an insurmountable amount of pressure on them to complete duties, many that are not in their job description. She tends to yell to get her point across and she likes to write them up when they do not comply with her seemingly unrealistic deadlines. One of the employees, Matthew is particularly displeased with Myrna's management style and verbal skills. He goes to her office one day to confront her on an incident that happened last week when she was highly upset with the team and began to berate them to the point where one of the employees left the meeting in tears. When he attempted to talk to Myrna, she immediately became upset and dismissed his and the other employees feelings. After the meeting, Matthew told his team members about his encounter with her and they all agreed to speak to her supervisor to intervene in the conflict between them. Unfortunately, Myrna's supervisor appeared to be uninterested in their complaint and told them that he is sure that Myrna can deal with whatever issues that they have with her on her own.

Employee and supervisor conflict can easily be resolved without intervention from upper management or conflict resolution consultation. However, far too often, organizations allow employee and supervisor conflict to get out of hand. There are various types of conflict that happens between employees and supervisors. One of the most common types of conflict is performance based; particularly during times of performance evaluations. The conflict arises when employees feel that their performance was unfairly evaluated by their supervisor. Both parties actually have a responsibility in diffusing this type of conflict. Supervisors have a responsibility of communicating their expectations to employees as early as possible, while employees have a responsibility of executing these expectations to the best of their ability. How conflict usually happens in this case is that supervisors fail to communicate their expectations early on and fail to provide feedback on employees' performance on a regular basis. As a result, employees never get an understanding on the areas in which they need to improve until the

*Healing in the Workplace*

performance evaluation and by this time, they are confused about the feedback that they receive. On the other hand, employees have a responsibility to periodically ask their supervisors to provide them with feedback on their performance. This will not only help them improve upon their skills but will show their supervisors that they are open to enhancing the work skills which ultimately helps the organization. One other employee and supervisor conflict is relational in nature. Some people just do not see eye-to-eye on things that have nothing to do with the job in and of itself. This occurs when people have personality differences or views things from differing perspectives. Even further, this can happen when either the employee, supervisor or both have poor social skills and have not learned to "play nice" with others. First Lady Hokes said that she believes that some people just have poor social and people skills that need to be improved. many can argue that this was the case in the vignette with Myrna because she would frequently yell to communicate her feelings to her subordinates and even became defensive when this was brought to her attention. In this instance, handling the conflict between the employee and supervisor is not so easy. In fact, Matthew in the vignette attempted to seek resolution by involving Myrna's supervisor when she was not open to listening to his concerns. Pastor Hokes said that he believes that Matthew went through the proper channels to get some intervention, but it was unfortunate that her supervisor was not willing to solve the problem. He said that he has seen that happen a lot in organizations because often times middle and upper management collude with one another instead of doing what is best for their employees. Employees have options if their supervisor fails to resolve the conflict. One of the problems; particularly for Christians in the workplace is that they overlook the conflict and fail to resolve it. Many of them may believe that the conflict with their supervisors will just go away or that God does not want them to stand up for themselves during conflict. Pastor Hokes said that Christians have to stop believing that they have to be a doormat and turn the other cheek when they are involved in conflict, even when it is with their supervisors. He said that Christians sometimes associate

*L'Orangerie Crawford & Terri Harrison*

humility with meekness; however it is our job as Christians to stand up for righteousness. He said that what we must remember is that God wants us to stand up for righteousness in the appropriate way. In Isaiah 1:17, the Bible tells us to learn to do good, seek justice, and rebuke oppressors. We must be proper in our methods to seek justice during conflict with our supervisors. First, we must attempt to meet with them to resolve the problem and if they are unwilling then we can attempt to resolve the problem ourselves. For example, if the conflict is over a work-related task such as confusion over a deadline, attempt to turn in the project as early as possible to avoid the supervisor becoming upset. Additionally, if the conflict is a result of interpersonal and personality issues then reduce as much interaction with the supervisor as possible. One of the ways to do this is by communicating through emails rather than engaging in face to face communication. This also helps when the dislike for a supervisor or employee will not just go away. First Lady Hokes said that many of us do not know what to do when we have to be around people that we just do not like and probably will never like. In this case, we have to maintain some distance between one another in order to avoid the conflict negatively affecting the work environment. Nonetheless, if we have to be around them then we must be mindful of our approach toward them. Pastor Hokes said that we must remember what the Bible says about acting out when we are angry. He said that James 1:19 tells us to be swift to hear and slow to anger. Once more, he said that we must remember that a soft answer turns away wrath. First Lady Hokes said that Christians need to pray and ask God to take the resentment out of their hearts for the person that they dislike. She said that we must consider that some people cannot handle the pressures that they are experiencing on their jobs and this causes them to act out at work. Having this understanding and asking God to help us be more compassionate does not mean that a sudden liking to the person will occur, but it will help ease some tension. If the appropriate measures have been taken and conflict still continues between employees and supervisors, then mediation from human resources or an outside

*Healing in the Workplace*

conflict manager may be the only means to diffuse any current and future problems.

Colleagues whom have conflict with one another can set a negative vibe among the team. Managers must be proactive in dealing with the conflict between colleagues, otherwise it can trickle down to other employees and impact morale. Managers must help colleagues manage conflict appropriately by prohibiting them to escape the conflict and deal with it hand on. Conflict can never be resolved if it is not addressed. Once more, managers must show employees that it is an opportunity confront one another in an empathetic manner. Pastor Hokes said that God uses conflict as teachable moments. He wants us to learn about ourselves when we are in conflict. Only then can we correct the negative traits that we have that contributes to the conflict.

## EMPLOYEE/EMPLOYEE CONFLICT:

Layla and Caroline are both senior executives at a small, neighborhood newspaper publishing company. Layla has newly migrated to the United States while Caroline is a born American. They both were introduced to one another by their boss because of their closely related job duties and because the boss thought that they would hit it off. Caroline would often tell jokes that did not go over well with Layla. She almost always had a confused look on her face after the joke was told and would just shrug her shoulders and walk out of the room. After several unacknowledged jokes by Layla, Caroline was perplexed and decided to tell Layla more jokes in hopes that she would come around. Caroline is used to receiving positive attention for her jokes and just could not understand why Layla did not get them. One day Caroline told a joke during a meeting that the other attendees laughed at but Layla dismissed. Caroline became highly offended and called her out on it right in front of the other people. She asked her: "Do you have a problem with what I am saying? Why don't you ever laugh at my jokes? You are

173

so stand offish!" Surprised by Caroline's reaction, Layla turned red and walked out of the room. Later on that day, Caroline's boss confronted her about the episode. She told Caroline that Layla did not laugh at any of her jokes because in her culture, it is a sign of disrespect to laugh at someone that is admired. Caroline felt so guilty. She did not realize that this was a cultural issue, not to mention that Layla actually admired her which is why she was not laughing at her. Caroline later apologized to Layla and asked for her forgiveness.

Most of the time we fail to communicate our true feelings during conflict; especially when we have conflict with our colleagues. Many times there is an underlying issue that is attributed to the conflict, but we have a difficult time communicating this to others. An example of this may be if a team in an organization frequently goes out to lunch but one member cannot attend because of a work commitment. This team member may feel left out but fail to communicate this to the rest of the team. Instead, she might be harsh when she communicates with them or distant toward them. This team member has an obligation to communicate her true feelings to her team members instead of behaving passive aggressively otherwise she is being deceitful. Many people behave in a passive aggressive manner during conflict for many reasons but do not realize what they are doing. Passive-aggressive behavior during conflict is when a person does not actively engage in the conflict, but engage in it behind the scenes. This behavior is just as negative and damaging as aggressive behavior because it is counterproductive and does not help resolve the issue. People whom respond passive aggressively during conflict are often in denial about their anger which is why they work so hard to suppress it. The interesting thing about this is that in the midst of them working so hard to suppress their anger, it is still being communicated without them even realizing it. Think about it. Imagine that one friend makes a comment that offends the other friend. This friend may be so offended that he ignores all of his friend's phone calls instead of simply just telling him that he was offended. The funny thing is that the friend who was offended does not realize that by ignoring

*Healing in the Workplace*

his friend's phone calls is communicating his anger toward him. This is actually another form of the "silent treatment" which is immature in God's eyes because it is not the way that adults should handle conflict. Often times people give others the "silent treatment" because they have yet to develop the appropriate coping skills to deal with their own anger about the conflict. What they are not realizing is that this type of behavior only adds to the problem. Even further, aggressive behavior during conflict is damaging as well. Aggressive behavior often acts as a defense mechanism to protect oneself from harm. In fact, research has shown that people tend to have three types of responses to danger or threat: flight, fight, or freeze. One of the authors reported that she has recognized that during conflict, her response tends to be to fight and has acknowledged this flaw as being unproductive and even destructive in her relationships with others. Most people whom respond with a fight response during conflict are actually very sensitive and watchful of harm from other people. In other words, in most cases these type of people do not like being hurt by others; especially if it is from others that they love and respect. Pastor Hokes said that people do not realize that harmful words or acts by someone stings more when it is from someone who we respect. This is why it is so important to constantly keep our words in check and be careful about what we say to others; particularly to our colleagues. Pastor Hokes said that this is why joke telling, like in the vignette is never appropriate in the workplace. He said that we have to be cognizant of what we say and how we say it because we never know who we may be offending. He also said that people do not realize that when we are speaking, others are actually listening; especially if we are claiming to be Christians. In fact, First Lady Hokes suggested that Christians are one of the most scrutinized group of people because we are to be the light in the midst of darkness. Pastor Hokes revealed that we cannot say any and everything that comes to our minds in the workplace; however many of us do this on a daily basis. This is because the Bible tells us that the tongue is the only member that is untamed. James 3:7-8 tells us that every beast on this earth can be tamed but the tongue is unruly and full of deadly poison in which no man can tame.

This is why God tells us that life and death *is* in the power of the tongue. In relationships, our words can speak life and we can have healthy relationships or our words can speak death and result in unhappiness in our relationships. We must be wise in our words to one another even when we are telling jokes. In the vignette, Caroline was unwise in her speech because not only did she make jokes that could have offended others, but she inappropriately confronted Layla in front of others. God knows that taming the tongue is one of the most difficult things to do; especially during conflict. However, one thing that we must realize is that if we do not control what we say to others during conflict, then we are acting against God's character if we profess to be Christians. One of the authors reported that she feels convicted about the times that she has failed to tame her tongue during conflict with others because she knows that it went against God. She also said that she realized that in those moments, she was actually giving Satan the victory because she was not exhibiting Christian-like behavior. First Lady Hokes said that we should always want people to have a godly vision and perception of us. Once more, Pastor Hokes said that we have to always consider the costs when we are in conflict with others. He said that Caroline needed to think about whether or not the reward to tell jokes was worth losing Layla's respect for her. We must model God's love in the workplace and remember that we are accountable to God for our actions during conflict with others. Like Pastor Hokes powerfully said, we have to behave properly during conflict because the softest pillow to sleep on is a clear conscious.

We have all heard of the saying that the customer is always right. Anyone who has worked in any form of customer services knows that clients can push buttons and induce anger. The reality is that customers are not always right, but store owners and staff are not always right either. Many people do not know what to do when they find themselves in conflict with a customer or a store owner or staff member. However, God gives us many examples of how to treat one another in these situations. One of the Bible's most appropriate examples of employee

*Healing in the Workplace*

and client conflict is tax collectors and their clients. These examples will be further examined in the text. The employee and client relationship is unique because it involves the exchange of money. God wants us to treat one another with respect when we exchange money for possessions. In fact, God gave the Israelites specific laws to abide by in Deuteronomy 23:19-20 when it came to the exchange of money because He wants us to be fair to one another during this process.

## EMPLOYEE/CLIENT CONFLICT:

Mickey and his family decided to do a little retail therapy one weekend. They went to the mall to buy some school supplies for the kids and some home goods. Mickey and his family walked into the store and instantaneously caught the attention of the store owners. They began closely watching him and his teenage sons in belief that they might steal something from the store. At first, Mickey did not notice that he was being followed by the store owners, but the more that Mickey and his boys looked at the merchandise, the less the store owners were discrete about watching them. Mickey's wife suddenly caught on and told him to round up the boys so that they could leave the store. Mickey and his family left the store, but was still being followed by the store owners. They would walk faster but the store owners would continue to follow them. One of the store owners shouted out that one of Mickey's sons stole a CD. Mickey and his family ran out of the mall and one of the store owners grabbed Mickey's son's backpack and tried to wrestle him to the ground. Mickey began cursing and yelling at the store owners and it appeared that they were going to get into a fight. The mall security eventually showed up at the scene and Mickey told him what just happened. The security guard asked Mickey's son to open his backpack and there was nothing in it. Unbeknownst to Mickey, his family, and the store owners, another customer saw the entire incident and told the security guard that the store owners were harassing and watching

Mickey and his family for no reason. She also said that she believes that Mickey and his family were racially profiled.

One of the most difficult jobs to have is customer service is because one has to put on a brave face and remain calm even when customers are berating them and behaving in a belligerent manner. One of the authors was reminded of a time that she worked as a customer service representative at a call center and had to deal with rude and offensive customers on a daily basis. She said that many of the clients would call her hurtful names and take their anger out on her. She reported that the stress from the interaction with these type of customers caused her to feel depressed. What is even more unfortunate about her experience is that she did not receive any support from her organization to help cope with the clients' aggressive behaviors. Organizations do their employees a disservice when they do not implement debriefing programs to help them cope with conflict with clients. In fact, managers need to be responsible for checking with their employees to find out how they are coping with clients' demands. One of the things that employees can do is learn how to manage their stress by exercising, sleeping and eating properly, and even joining a support group or forming a support group at work to talk about the conflict with customers. On the flip side of this, customers can also be treated badly by staff and store owner like Mickey and his family were in the vignette. As mentioned earlier in the text, the Bible references the conflict between tax collectors and the people because they were considered to be thieves and traitors. During this time, Rome occupied Israel's land and collected taxes for the Roman empire which is why the Jews hated tax collectors. Although it was the tax collector's job to collect money, many of the Jews felt that they were treated unfairly by them. Many of the tax collectors brought false charges against the people and attempted to extort money from them. Because of this, the tax collectors were instructed in Luke 3:13 to collect no more than what is appointed. God dislikes it when store owners or staff mistreat customers. One of the ways in which customers are unfairly treated is through racial profiling. Mickey and

*Healing in the Workplace*

his family were racially profiled by the store owners which caused a near physical altercation. This form of mistreatment is racism at its core because it is classifying a group of people in a negative manner based off of unproven claims. Many store owners whom engage in this type of behavior actually think that they are better than the customers and that the customers should not be in their store. Pastor Hokes said that God despises this type of treatment toward others because it is arrogant. He said that in Romans 12:3, the Bible instructs us to not think of too highly of ourselves than we ought to think. Even further, God does not want us to think too highly of ourselves that we begin to think less of others. This is exactly what is happening when store owners falsely accuse their customers of stealing or not belonging in their store because of their race. Pastor Hokes said that racial profiling is alive and well but we must have a strategy to combat it. He said that we cannot deny nor ignore it, but we must fight back. He said that one of the ways in which we can fight against racial profiling is to behave intelligently and properly when we are in stores so that we do not bring negative attention to ourselves and give store owners or staff a reason to assume that we are unworthy of shopping in their store. This does not mean that we must conform and be something that we are not, but we as customers have an obligation to behave appropriately when we are shopping in someone's store because owners have worked hard to obtain their businesses and we must respect that. Business owners must remember that without the support of their clients, they would not have a viable business. Therefore, they must treat them with respect. At the same time, customers must realize that store owners have the right to refuse service to them if they are brooding conflict. Therefore, they must also treat the business with respect. The bottom line is that God desires that we treat one another with respect when we are in one another's presence. Jesus was our perfect example of how to treat one another even in the midst of conflict when He was dying on the cross, but still asked God to forgive His persecutors. We must be like Jesus and cope with conflict more appropriately and forgive one another just like God forgives us for our sins.

*L'Orangerie Crawford & Terri Harrison*

## THINGS TO PONDER ON:

- When a supervisor communicates poorly to staff through verbal out-lash such behavior is unprofessional, demeaning, and mean-spirited. Supervisors undoubtedly have a difficult role of managing many personalities; however they have a responsibility to humble themselves as the Lord teaches in Phillippians to think of others before yourself. It is time for true conviction, change dangerous behavior patterns, and stop provoking/bullying others...........Phillippians 2:1-4 NKJV

- Many times supervisors fall in a trap of deception of believing they have a right to speak to a subordinate in any fashion they please because they are in charge. But, they have been deceived by Satan and it is a trick of the enemy as pride and self righteousness has taken root in the spirit. If you are a supervisor do you disrespect yourself and others by talking down to subordinates? Do you believe you can continue to mistreat subordinates and go unscathed? Consider heeding the Lord's directive "do all things without complaining and disputing, that you may become blameless and harmless, children of God without fault in the midst of a crooked and perverse generation, among whom you shine as lights in the world, holding fast the word of life, so that I may rejoice in the day of Christ that I have not run in vain or labored in vain.......Phillippians 2:14-16 NJKV

- Employee-Employee conflict will never cease in the workplace but it is manageable. Oft, reasons coworkers fall out with one another usually is caused by silly half truths spread through the rumor mill. A simple solution is to stop paying attention to what others are doing and saying if it does not directly have any bearing on your job performance or productivity. Confession and asking for forgiveness is the initial step with moving forward

*Healing in the Workplace*

peacefully. However, this does not always mean both parties will be singing "kum ba ya" and become best of friends; but it lets one another off the hook and may even save them from losing their job. The bible says, "Take heed to yourselves. If your brother sins against you, rebuke him; and if he repents, forgive him".......Luke 17:3 NKJV

- Eliminate conflict among employees through corrective interventions; for example bring parties together with a project. Interventions are great tools as they are effective in breaking down barriers associated to communication problems. For the most part employee conflict is stemmed from not knowing one another evidenced by low morale running rampant throughout the workplace. People must have a sense of who they are working side-by-side in order to build mutual respect. Creating monthly projects where the team is paired off to present on a work-related topic is a good way to start dialog. Pair together the party who has had conflict by directing them to compare and contrast a job issue needing improvement. Upon completion openly reward their efforts. Consider the word of God, "that there should be no schism in the body, but that the members should have the same care for one another. And if one member suffers, all the members suffer with it; or if one member is honored, all the members rejoice with it"..............I Corinthians 12:25-26 NJKV

- Retailers have a right to protect their goods from theft but not at the expense of accusing patrons of thievery based off of a stereotype or mere following the patron around throughout the store. Business owners must operate under the guides of trustworthiness if they want to survive. Yes, there are patrons whose intention is to steal upon entry but overall it makes no sense to go overboard in policing and protecting goods and services. On the contrary, this type of business tactic can

181

cause physical violence and/or litigation. It is best to come to a quick resolution as the word tells us "agree with your adversary quickly, while you are on the way with him, lest your adversary deliver you to the judge, the judge hand you over to the officer, and you be thrown into prison"...........Matthew 5:25 NKJV

- Before rendering a judgment upon an offense it is vital in being fair to gather as much facts as possible. Immediately, jumping to conclusions taints due process towards fair and equitable treatment. Employers have a legal responsibility to ensure their employees are not being harmed while performing their customary duties. For example, examine a call-center employee who receives enormous amount of calls per day but the percentage of rude, obnoxious and harassing calls taken is harmful. Unfortunately, most managers would not and/or do not think the employee is being harassed. Meanwhile, these types of work environments have a high number of workers' compensation cases, stress cases, and employees eventually become bitter and callous towards the client. If you are a manager create a safe haven for the employee to debrief do not pass judgment and say it is in the scope of the employee duties to accept harassment from a client. It is wrong to pass judgment as we are told in the book of John "do not judge according to appearance, but judge with righteous judgment"...........John 7:24 NKJV

# SERVANTHOOD

It is fitting to conclude, "Healing in the workplace" with Servitude as God admonishes the mean-spirited supervisor, the workplace gossiper, and others previously depicted to change and walk upright before him and others.

- Servanthood means employees and employers work in unison with a common goal to reach an end result. Both are directed to not perform any task for self ambition but to serve each other with humility (Phil 2:3-4) God expects each person to be interdependent and dependent on him solely.

- God has given man his format for living a successful life while serving others for the purpose of advancing the kingdom of God. When man goes against biblical principles or fails to seek biblical instruction, this is the beginning of a problematic life.

- Man was created to serve God and to have an attitude of servanthood in showing God's love for the world. The bible tells us in Luke we are duty bound to serve with gratitude and not to serve to be seen but out of reverence and fulfillment to God's command. In other words, employees and supervisors are too work together in harmony, walk in love toward one another, speak highly of each other, and humbly serve each other (Phil 2:1-4).

183

*L'Orangerie Crawford & Terri Harrison*

- As Jesus showed the example of being a good servant by washing the feet of his disciples, supervisors are to humble themselves to their staff and ensure their staff is equipped with every tool necessary to conducting an excellence job performance (John 13:12-17).

- Likewise, employees are to submit to authority of their supervisor, meaning to respect the position the supervisor holds as it is the mantle of leadership. God understands not all supervisors themselves understand the position they are permitted to fulfill which is the primary reason most abuse occurs.

- However, assuming a supervisor does not have an understanding of their leadership mantle God still expects subordinates to honor the position. Importantly, God calls supervisors to treat employees fairly and equitably as well. God holds supervisors accountable to him for the type of service he/she gives to employees.

- Healing is critical to eradicate workplace woes. Because of sin man tills the land; but God never intended work to be complicated, on the contrary, he set life in order to bless, all provision was for the asking with continuous flow.

- Workplace woes can reduce once all members take on the mindset, that of serving their fellow coworker (Matt 20:27-28) as true leadership means serving. The concept of leadership seems to never be equated to that of servant.

- In contrast, successful leaders understand their ability to lead is contingent upon their ability to serve the people humbly with a willing heart. It is important to evaluate ourselves asking if we are serving our coworkers as Jesus did. Is any job beneath our

*Healing in the Workplace*

scope when asked by leadership to perform a duty not in the job description?

- Healing is not impossible and working in a stress-free workplace is possible; but it will take commitment from management to serve the staff and staff to support management.

- Another form of servanthood calls for coworkers to be obedient and have a desire to do for others openly. It is time to move away from "it's all about me" mentality and embrace the attitude of community which includes involvement of everyone.

- Workers serve each other in love (Gal 5:13)

- Workers who want to promote must be willing to serve everyone (Mark 9:35)

- Managers treat staff justly even when no one is watching for God is always watching and holding accountability to him and will repay for unjust treatment to subordinates (Luke 12:45-47)

- Managers equip staff for service (Luke 6:40)

- Managers must have a servant heart to lead and gain respect of subordinates (Mark 10:42-45)

# L'Orangerie Crawford, MA, MFTI

L'Orangerie Crawford is a trained Marriage and Family Therapist Intern and has been a practicing Christian since she was 10 years old. She has worked with many children and families in inner city communities and has conducted research on issues in community mental health. She lives in Los Angeles, California and has recently had a baby girl in the winter of 2012! This is her first published book.

She is currently receiving a Doctorate degree in Business Psychology with an emphasis on Consulting from The Chicago School of Professional Psychology-LA Campus and is dedicating her dissertation research to examining the impact of slavery on modern day African Americans in the workplace. She also received a Masters Degree in Psychology from Phillips Graduate Institute in Encino, California and a Bachelors of Arts degree from the University of Southern California in Los Angeles, California.

L'Orangerie is a dedicated follower of Jesus Christ and has always wanted to combine her education and field of expertise with the word of God. She was inspired to co-author this book along with her mother, Terri L. Harrison, MAED because they have discerned that most people have challenges in their workplace but do not know how to cope with them from a spiritual perspective.

After graduating with her Doctorate degree in 2014, she plans on consulting with businesses in an array of areas including strategic planning, consumer marketing, conflict resolution and management, training and development, and recruitment and selection. Once more, she has a passion for teaching others and plans on pursuing a teaching career.

# Terri L. Harrison, MAED, BSBM

Terri L. Harrison is a doctoral student of Business Psychology, emphasis on Industrial Organization Consulting at The Chicago School of Professional Psychology, Los Angeles. She received her MAED from Argosy University, Orange and her BSBM from University of Phoenix, Culver City and afterwards eventually co found two family owned businesses. She brings a myriad of experience derived from over 28 years of governmental service in unemployment, legal services, construction engineering, labor compliance contracts, health and safety, workers' compensation, and right-of-way. Ms. Harrison recently collaborated on a manuscript with her daughter L'Orangerie A. Crawford, doctoral student of Business Psychology, I/O Consulting, MA, entitled Healing in the workplace. Ms. Harrison and Ms. Crawford decided to follow their passion and call compiling issues within the workplace as they saw a desperate cry out for help from employees and employers on how to address legitimate and sensitive issues within the workplace from a spiritual perspective.

In addition, Ms. Harrison is a purpose coach in which she has utilized her knowledge to guide others to discovery of purpose, proper tracking, and accomplishment. Upon receiving her doctorate degree she aspires to teach and consult with businesses in the areas of recruitment and selection, group facilitation, mediation, emotional intelligence, strategic planning, consumer marketing, conflict resolution and management, and training and development. Ms. Harrison is a member of the West Los Angeles Chamber of Commerce. She currently resides in Los Angeles with her family.

# Pastor Timothy Hokes

Dr. Timothy Hokes is the devoted husband of Evangelist Johnita Hokes, and father of 2 daughters, Johnita and Mazie. Dr. Hokes gave his life to God in April of 1981; after 20 plus years of ministry he received his mandate from God, Dr. Hokes obediently fulfilled his calling from God and is the Pastor of "The Key of David Ministries" Dr. Hokes received his "Doctorate of Ministry Degree" from "Rhemalife Theological Seminary". Dr. Hokes has a tremendous passion for God's word coupled with a love for God's people he has a contagious spirit of generosity that flows through every facet of his ministry, His vision is uncompromisingly clear with one central principle, to provide a church where people along with their families can have a continual-life changing experience with God.

Dr. Hokes contact information: The Key of David, 15507 South Normandie Ave, Suite 433, Gardena, California 90247, Telephone: (323) 543-5212.

# First Lady Johnita Hokes

First Lady Johnita Hokes co pastors along side her husband Dr. Timothy Hokes of The Key of David Ministries. She has two daughters Johnita and Mazie Hokes. She is a licensed Evangelist and earned her Bachelor Degree in Teaching with an emphasis in mathematics from Cal State Dominquez Hills.

First Lady was saved as a teenager and found at an early age that living for God was the best course for her life. She has served in many capacities in the church, i.e. Usher Board, Young Women Christian Counsel, Mission Department, and a Sunday School teacher just to name a few.

Johnita is gifted in teaching and is now currently working diligently with her husband of 25 years in the building of the Kingdom Of God. First Lady loves God and has a genuine love for His people.

Made in the USA
Lexington, KY
11 August 2018